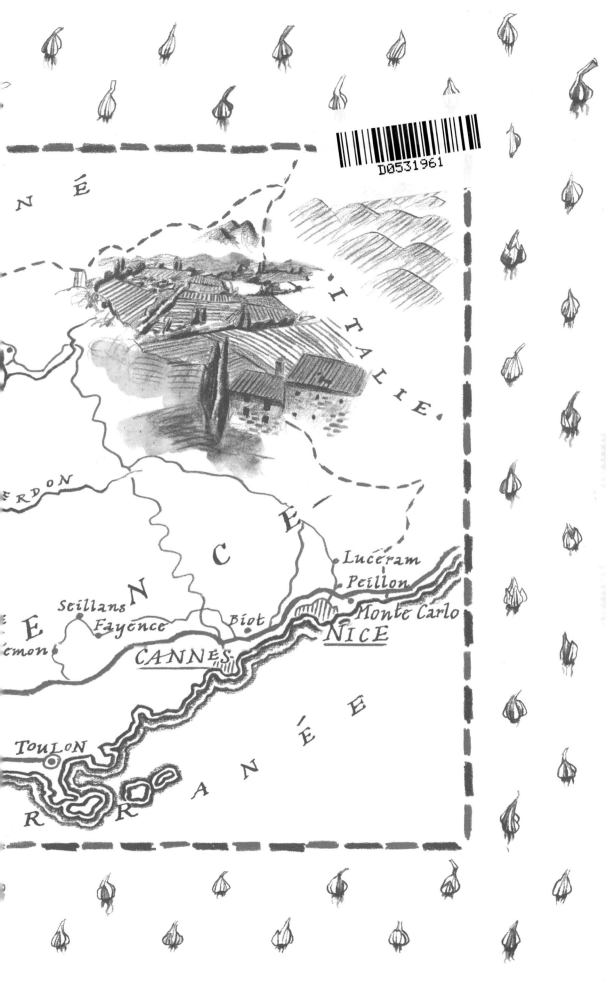

A TASTE OF
· PROVENCE ·

To ANDREW THOMAS
for his quarts of tea & gallons of advice,
•
To Gabrielle, Ann & Lorraine
for their infinite patience,
•
and to everyone in Provence who made this
book possible –
my second family at Les Bastides,
Jill & Suzy in Nice, Louisa in Avignon, Jo & Annick
in Vaison, André in Marseilles.

A · Taste · of
PROVENCE

Classic Recipes from the South of · France ·

Collected & Illustrated by Leslie Forbes

BARNES
& NOBLE
BOOKS
NEW YORK

First hardback edition published in the United States by
Little Brown & Co.
First paperback edition published in the United States by
Chronicle Books

This edition published by Barnes & Noble, Inc. by
arrangement with Gardenhouse Designs Ltd.

2001 Barnes & Noble Books

M 10 9 8 7 6 5 4 3 2 1

Printed in Singapore by Kyodo Printing Co. Pte. Ltd.

Library of Congress Cataloging-in-Publication Data:
Forbes, Leslie.
    A taste of Provence: classic recipes from the south of France/
collected and illustrated by Leslie Forbes.
        p. cm.
    Includes index.
    ISBN 0-7607-2631-0
    1. Cookery, French–Provencal-style.   2. Provence (France)-
- Description and travel.   I. Title.

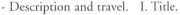

· CONTENTS ·

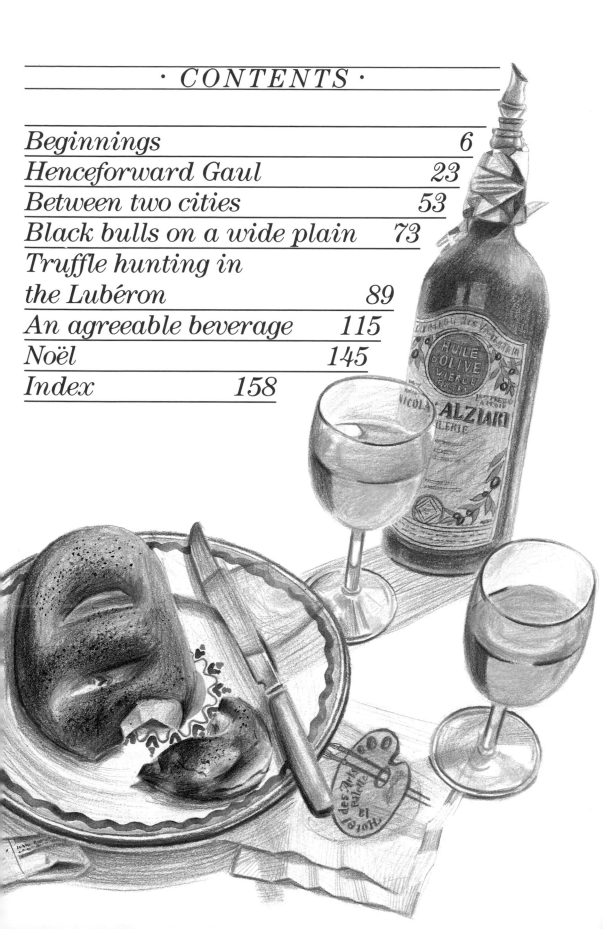

BEGINNINGS

'the same cicadas sang in Caesar's reign,
upon the walls the same sun clings and climbs.'
Vladimir Nabokov (1899–1977)

My first home in Provence, if home can be called a state of mind rather than a place of long residence, was a Bed & Breakfast – what the French call a Chambre d'Hôte – in an old windmill whose sails had long ceased turning. My blue-shuttered window looked south across vineyards & silver olive trees to the ruined town of Oppède-le-Vieux that clung half-way up the slopes of the Lubéron mountain. The peace was disturbed only by a few lazy flies, by the weekend baying of hunting dogs (it was autumn, when the primitive hunting spirit in all good Provençal men wakes up) & by the early-morning grinding of gears in my 70-year-old landlady's ancient & venerable Citroën. It was weeks before I discovered that every morning at six Madame Bonnet had driven 15 kilometres to the next village to buy fresh croissants for my breakfast. "Because Mademoiselle is something of a connoisseur, hein? And the bread in our village is acceptable, but the croissants no." Later I persuaded Madame Bonnet to trade the croissants for a handful of her muscat grapes & a few sun-ripened figs picked off the garden tree.

The walls of Madame Bonnet's old windmill were of thick stone, which had once been plastered but had peeled reg-

ularly enough over the years to build up a pleasantly textured landscape. A few massively-framed ancestral photographs, once brightly hand-tinted but now faded, hung in the spaces between heavy furniture & windows. And over every inch of horizontal space, barring beds & a few square feet of floor, crowded bottles of preserves – homemade fruit wines & eye-wateringly powerful eaux-de-vie, olive oils & vinegars with mysterious tentacled herbs waving in their depths, olives, wild mushrooms, cherries & pickled plums. These bottles were Madame Bonnet's treasure, & her insurance against lonely winters. For me they were the first insight into an older Provence, not our modern vision of a sun-drenched country permanently at lunch under the plane trees, but of a harsher country, where the summer's abundant fruits needed to be conserved against a more frugal winter, and where the gathering of wild herbs & vegetables was a necessity rather than a hobby.

The Provençal people are an adaptable race – they have gained a lot from the foreigners who have colonized their country over the past couple of thousand years. From the Greeks, who arrived by boat to found Massalia (Marseilles) in 600 BC, the Provençals got the olive, and swiftly turned it into an oil that far surpassed that of its country of origin. The Romans arrived later & on foot, but they stamped Provence with a firmer print than the Greeks, even calling it their province – 'Provincia'. More than just a name stuck: the Romans left behind some of their greatest cities – Nîmes, Arles, Orange, all still with spectacular Roman monuments today – as well as a taste for the strangely spiced sauces that still give Provençal cooking a pungent, earthy quality unlike any other in France. Anchoïade, the thick anchovy paste made with pounded olive oil, vinegar & garlic, brings with it more than a whiff of the Roman fish sauce called garum that was mixed with everything from mustard seed to anise. The Provençal habit of serving lots of little vegetable appetizers probably came east with the Spanish Moors, as did the preference for saffroned rice rather than potatoes.

It wasn't only the Romans who left a taste for Italian food in Provence. Nice joined Italy's House of Savoy in 1388 & wasn't re-attached to France until 1860, by which time polenta & pasta were firmly established in the south-east Provençal diet. The cuisine continued to change, picking up the cooking of tourists and colonists and adding essential local ingredients – dried orange peel, olive oil, garlic, thyme and basil, fennel and anise, anchovies and saffron and tomatoes – to give each new dish a taste of an older Provence. It is difficult now to say where classic Provençal cuisine really begins. Certainly the use of olive oil instead of butter is one great constant, and so is the emphasis on vegetables instead of meat – until 1914 the poorer Provençal families ate meat, at most, once a week. Most of the more lavish recipes that appeared in so-called 'Provençal' cookbooks at the turn of this century cater for the comfortable bourgeois families of the Riviera and the bigger provincial towns, not for country kitchens in the hilltop villages of northern Provence.

*T*he real Provençal cuisine was essentially lived and spoken, but not written down. It remains in the memories and long-established habits of grandmothers like Madame Bonnet, and in the country's more remote towns, where tourists with a dislike of garlic seldom stray.

*I*f old stones could be squeezed of their secrets like old grapes, then Madame Bonnet's farmhouse could reveal Provence as it was 70 years ago and more, before electricity and the paved road changed it for good.

· ONE DAY IN AN OLD KITCHEN ·

*T*he kitchen is the heart, the hub, the only big room in the house. In the room next to it are the stalls where the horses stand, their warm animal noises comforting on the days when the mistral fills the air with a whirlwind of dust, dead leaves & grapes. The north wall is blind against this fierce wind but it still manages sometimes to wrench the shutters from south-facing windows & blow the lace curtains flat against the ceiling. Fortunately the mistral does not blow all year round. In summer it is only a rustle of dried herbs over the red tiled floor.

· LE PETIT DÉJEUNER ·

The men start work early on summer mornings, at about five or six, but are back in three hours to eat 'à la fourchette' eggs and cheese, or gratins left over from last night's supper. The women make do with large bowls of café au lait in which to dip bread smeared with homemade jam, usually fig or watermelon. There is a saying in Provence, 'It's best to eat figs in the morning – by evening they are not so digestible.'

· CONFITURE de FIGUES · SÈCHES au JUS de RAISIN

dried fig & grape juice jam (to make about 1½ lb/750 g jam)

Figs, grapes, apples and mushrooms are strung up & dried for the winter in the kitchen's huge stone fireplace – next to hams, smoking over a chestnut fire. When sugar is too costly, jams are made from both dried and fresh fruits boiled in strong sweep grape juice. This one, with its delicious crunch of fig seeds, is very good on flat, crusty Fougasse bread straight from the oven.

12 OZ/350 G DRIED FIGS, CHOPPED

1¾ PT/1 LITRE PURE UNSWEETENED
  RED GRAPE JUICE

1 BOUQUET GARNI OF MINT, THYME
  AND MARJORAM

SHREDDED ZEST AND JUICE OF
  1 LEMON

1 VANILLA POD

UP TO 3 OZ/75 G SUGAR (OPTIONAL)

Soak the figs for 2 hours in the juice. Strain juice into a wide, heavy-based saucepan with the bouquet garni & reduce by half over high heat. Lower heat, add figs, lemon zest & vanilla pod, remove bouquet garni, & simmer very gently until fruit is tender (about 1–1½ hours). Remove vanilla, stir in lemon juice & test for sweetness – you may wish to add sugar. Boil rapidly, stirring often, just until setting point is reached (from 3–7 mins), but be careful not to over-cook, as the liquid evaporates quickly and over-boiling will make the jam sticky & tasteless. Jam is cooked when a drop of it on a cold saucer wrinkles sluggishly (but doesn't run) when tipped on its side. Remove from heat, let stand until tepid and pour into cleaned and dried jars. Cover & seal when cool. It is best to refrigerate this jam after opening.

*T*he main meal of the day is at noon but the Casse-croûte (which means literally 'breaking the crust') staves off pangs of mid-morning hunger. It may be a rolled herb omelette, soup in a flask or a chunk of strong cheese – 'Lou Cachat' – on crusty bread. Those with noses and palates of cast-iron wash this pungent cheese down with a glass of the eau-de-vie in which it has fermented.

• Bay •

LOU CACHAT
crushed cheese

BAY LEAVES DIPPED IN
    OLIVE OIL
GOAT CHEESES
COGNAC OR EAU DE VIE
BLACK PEPPER, ROUGHLY
    CRUSHED
FRESH SAVORY

The Provençal poet Frédéric Mistral, born in 1830, was a great chronicler of the country's traditions. Around him has grown up a romantic cult – the Félibrige – who record his every thought (he wrote only in Provençal) on subjects that range from the influence of Provençal troubadours on Dante's poetry to the right way to cook Provençal daube. Mistral calls Lou Cachat 'fragrant cheese', but its acerbic charm does more to clear the nostrils than perfume them.

• Savory •

Line an earthenware jar with bay leaves and press layers of goat cheese into it. Over each layer sprinkle several spoonfuls of cognac, a teaspoon of pepper and several sprigs of savory. Seal with more cognac and leave for at least 3 days in a cool place but not a refrigerator. Top up with more ingredients as you use it. It will last forever, but beware the last layer could be breathtakingly strong!

The midday meal is often a Bajane – a big pot filled with water, dried vegetables such as chickpeas, lentils or dried beans from the dark, cool storeroom next to the kitchen, and maybe a sausage or two. It's first boiled over the fire and then simmered all morning over the embers while the women work. When the men arrive home the vegetables ('la Bajane') are scooped out and tossed in vinaigrette and the sausage is sliced into the broth ('la Soupe'). The two dishes are served separately. With this there may be a salad of wild herbs that the women have collected – dandelions, rocket (arugola) and hyssop washed free of stubborn bugs under the handpump outside. In summer there are sweet peppers and aubergines cooked with garlic in the fireplace. And always lots of bread to eat with little homemade goats' cheeses laid out on bay leaves in flat rush baskets.

· Dandelion ·

· Carrot ·

· Rocket ·

· Spinach ·

· Borage ·

LA BAJANE de POIS CHICHES

*chickpea salad
with its own soup (6)*

The advantage of a Bajane is that from one pot you get two dishes, both distinct and subtly good. This version, where the nutty taste of chickpeas is mixed with Aïoli – unctuous garlic mayonnaise – makes a rich festive dish. For a more frugal meal substitute a good vinaigrette.

· LA BAJANE ·

1 LB/450 G CHICKPEAS SOAKED
   OVERNIGHT IN WATER WITH
   1 TSP/5ML BICARBONATE OF SODA
4 LEEKS

1 CARROT
5–6 SPINACH LEAVES
   (OPTIONAL, BUT
   THEY DO HELP
   SOFTEN THE PEAS)
2 CLOVES GARLIC
1 BAY LEAF
5 SAGE LEAVES
1 LARGE LEAN SAUSAGE
   OR 6 SMALL ONES
¼ TSP/1.25 ML NUTMEG
SALT & PEPPER
2 TBSP/30 ML FRESH
   PARSLEY, FINELY
   CHOPPED (FOR GARNISH)
3 OZ/75 G FRESH PASTA
GRATED GRUYÈRE
   (OPTIONAL)

(continued next page)

· AÏOLI ·

garlic mayonnaise

6–12 CLOVES FRESH GARLIC,
    PEELED & CHOPPED

1 EGG YOLK, BEATEN

9 FL OZ/275 ML (APPROX) GOOD
    OLIVE OIL

JUICE OF ½ LEMON

1 TSP/5 ML (APPROX) TEPID WATER

After soaking the peas rinse
them well in several changes
of water and drain. Put them
in a large saucepan with 6 pints
of cold water, two leeks and
the carrot, all cut into easily
retrievable pieces, the spinach
leaves (which serve to soften
the chickpeas), garlic, bay leaf
and sage. Bring slowly to
the boil, skim off any
scum, cover tightly &
simmer gently for 2–3
hours until the peas are
very tender.

About half an hour
before they are
cooked add the
sausage to the
chickpeas &
make

the aïoli. Mash the garlic to a
smooth paste in a marble or
ceramic mortar. Stir in the egg
yolk and begin adding the oil,
drop by drop first, then, when
it begins to thicken, in a steady
stream, beating constantly.
When the eggs have absorbed
about half the oil, add the
lemon juice and water and
continue slowly adding the
oil. If the mixture becomes
too thick before all
the oil has
been
added
pour
in a

few more drops of tepid water before continuing. Season with salt & pepper. When chickpeas & sausage are cooked remove them from the broth. Remove cooked vegetables from chickpeas, then mix peas with the aïoli, 1 raw sliced leek, nutmeg, salt & pepper to taste. Garnish with chopped parsley. Strain the broth, slice the sausage & add it to the broth with the remaining leek (finely sliced), the pasta, pepper and salt. Cook until the pasta is just tender. Sprinkle

with grated Gruyère if desired before serving.

In Marseilles the cooks say that a mortar & pestle should always smell of garlic.

· SALADE de POIVRONS ·
sweet pepper salad (6)

Grilling the peppers to remove their skins helps give this simple but decorative salad a subtly sweet taste that contrasts interestingly with the piquancy of the olives.

3-4 SWEET PEPPERS, MIXED RED,
   GREEN & YELLOW

3 TBSP/45 ML OLIVE OIL

1 TBSP/15 ML TARRAGON
   VINEGAR OR LEMON JUICE

HANDFUL FRESH THYME OR
   BASIL, ROUGHLY CHOPPED

SALT & PEPPER

GENEROUS HANDFUL OF RIPE
   BLACK OLIVES

Heat the peppers over a flame or under a hot grill, turning frequently, until all the skin blisters and can be easily peeled off. This is a fiddly process but worth it. Remove the peppers' stems and seeds and cut in thin strips lengthwise. Toss together with all the other ingredients and leave in a warm place for 1–2 hours. Toss again just before serving.

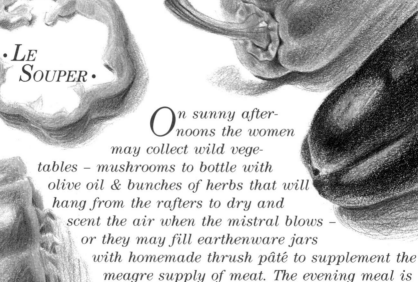

· LE SOUPER ·

*O*n sunny afternoons the women may collect wild vegetables – mushrooms to bottle with olive oil & bunches of herbs that will hang from the rafters to dry and scent the air when the mistral blows – or they may fill earthenware jars with homemade thrush pâté to supplement the meagre supply of meat. The evening meal is prepared in the morning: eggs, still warm from the hens, are cooked in a big omelette, to be covered in cheese & reheated over the fire later; gratins of vegetables are salted with a few anchovies; Lou Cachat is dug, protesting, out of its deep jar; a bowl of local cherries cooked in lavender honey is spooned over soft fromage frais.

·La Brandade de Haricots· aux Artichauts

haricot bean purée with artichokes

(serves 6 as a starter or as one of a group of main dishes)

On Fridays a shrivelled, unappetizing greyish strip of salt cod is taken off its hook to be placed in a small straw basket (covered against too-interested cats), soaked in the village fountain, pounded with olive oil & finally transformed into a near-legendary dish, Brandade de Morue. On fish-free days a creamy brandade of white beans may be prepared in the same way, and served with tiny violet artichokes simmered in wine and herbs, and perhaps even paper-thin slices of truffle over the top adding their inimitable rich, earthy scent.

ARTICHOKES:

12 BABY ARTICHOKES WITHOUT
   CHOKES, OR 6 LARGER ONES

JUICE OF ½ LEMON (1½ IF USING
   LARGE ARTICHOKES)

2 LEEKS, FINELY CHOPPED

OLIVE OIL

BOUQUET GARNI OF THYME,
   BAY & SAVORY

¼ TSP/1.25 ML CINNAMON

SALT & PEPPER

12 FL OZ/350 ML WHITE WINE

If using baby artichokes, simply remove any tough outer leaves and trim off just enough stem to allow the artichokes to stand upright. If using larger ones, have ready a bowl of cold water into which you have squeezed the juice of half a lemon. Prepare the artichokes one by one by trimming the stems, removing the tough outer leaves, then cutting the artichokes across about ½ in/1.5 cm from the bottom and scooping out the choke with a teaspoon. As you work, rub the juice from the extra lemon (cut in half) on to each artichoke heart to prevent it (continued on next page) from going black. Check there are no tough pieces attached to the heart and put it to soak in the cold water while you prepare the others.

In a large heavy casserole cook the leeks and garlic in a little oil until softened. Pack the artichokes and herbs on top tightly, sprinkle with cinnamon, salt, pepper and olive oil. Pour over the wine, add just enough water to cover and bring to a very low boil. Cover and cook for 20–25 minutes. When the artichokes are tender, remove them and reduce the broth by half to three-quarters.

• BRANDADE •

12 OZ/350 G WHITE HARICOT
  BEANS SOAKED OVERNIGHT

BOUQUET GARNI

2–3 CLOVES GARLIC, CRUSHED

6 FL OZ/175 ML BEST OLIVE OIL

2–3 FL OZ/50–75 ML MILK

JUICE OF ½ LEMON

SALT & PEPPER

12 CROÛTONS MADE FROM SMALL
  SLICES OF FRENCH BREAD

Rinse the beans well in running water and discard any skins. Put the beans in a heavy-based saucepan with the bouquet garni and cover with water. It should cover the beans by about an inch. Heat to boiling, boil for 5 minutes, reduce the heat and simmer very gently, tightly covered, for about 3 hours or until the beans are tender but not mushy. Pass through a sieve or purée in an electric blender. Beat in the garlic with a wooden sppon and over a low heat begin to beat in the oil, as you would with mayonnaise. About half-way through, start adding alternate dribbles of milk (heated just to boiling). For a less rich dish you can substitute some of the artichoke broth for the oil.

Finish off the dish with lemon juice and season with salt and pepper. Spoon the brandade into the centre of a large dish and scatter with croûtons. Pile the artichokes around the edge and moisten with the reduced broth, first strained. (The leeks can be served on top of the brandade if you like.) For a really special occasion scatter the top with truffle shavings or matchstick strips of smoked ham instead of croûtons.

· LA VEILLÉE ·

La Veillée – the evening gathering in front of the fire, the traditional time for gossip & chat. Men and women sort dried vegetables at the table, and swat the children – who burn their fingers on roasted chestnuts. There is a warm jug of Piquette, the poor man's substitute for wine – made with fermented grapeskins that have already been through a first pressing – that 'piques' or gives a lift. If the need is less for stimulation than relaxation, a bowl of tisane is easily made, sweetened with a spoonful of honey.

· TISANES ·
herbal teas

In Provence people have a not unfounded faith in the benefit of home-brewed herbal teas. Qualified doctors, instead of resorting to other medicines, are likely to prescribe tisanes for the relief of minor ailments. Four herbs in particular have been used effectively for centuries: sage, as an antiseptic for sore throats; verveine (verbena), for digestion and as a mild sedative; thyme, as a natural disinfectant to clean the system; and tilleul (lime), whose blossoms cure constipation and aid sleep.

To make a soothing tisane: place a small branch (5–6 leaves) of herbs into 2 pints/1 litre (approx) of cold water. Bring to the boil, cover & remove from heat. Let stand 5–10 mins before drinking. This can also be bottled, or scented at boiling point with:

a strip of orange peel

2–3 cloves

1 vanilla pod

a tbsp of acacia honey.

*I*n fine weather lunch is outside under the old
lime tree that snows blossoms when the wind
rustles. It is a feast day, one long delicious meal.
There may be a Grand Aïoli: a huge stone mortar
overflowing with yellow aïoli and surrounded
by bowls of petits gris snails cooked in stock,
poached salt cod, matchsticks of wild asparagus
and green beans, chickpeas and tiny waxen
potatoes. There is the local rosé wine, chilled
in the fountain, slices of smoky mountain
ham, hard-boiled eggs stuffed with Tapenado
– a peppery purée of olives and capers – and
   gleaming stone jars of wild mushrooms –

*lactaires délicieuses, chanterelles and
giant cèpes. If there is no aïoli, there is for once a
dish of meat: roast lamb studded with garlic and anchovies;
metre-length spits of tiny birds; plump chickens or wild hare
simmered in wine, the sauce thickened with blood; Provençal
stew – daube of mutton or beef, bubbling from dawn with
strips of dried orange peel. The meal finishes with a caramellized pumpkin pudding or a shimmering custard. The women
doze in the shade, to be wakened only by the crack-crack of
the men playing boules (called pétanque here).*

· CIVET de LIÈVRE ·
jugged hare (6)

*(Rabbit can be substituted for
hare in this recipe but the
quantities should be altered
accordingly.)*

*Aline Bouquet's grandmother
used to make this musky stew
at her little auberge in Viens.
Without the blood it is still a
good dish but lacks the characteristic gamy taste that
makes it so memorable. Don't
be tempted to use a strong
wine – the dish should taste
of the meat, not of alcohol.*

1 4 LB/1.8–2 KG HARE, SKINNED,
 CLEANED & CUT IN PIECES,
 LIVER RESERVED

BLOOD FROM THE HARE MIXED
 WITH 1 TSP/5 ML VINEGAR
 (CAN BE OMITTED BUT TASTES
 VERY GOOD)

1 BOTTLE RED WINE (NOT MORE
 THAN 11–12% ALCOHOL)

3–4 CLOVES GARLIC, PEELED &
 CRUSHED

2 LARGE ONIONS, PEELED AND
 THINLY SLICED

1 BOUQUET GARNI OF 2 BAY
 LEAVES, FRESH THYME AND
 SAVORY

7 OZ/220 G UNSMOKED BACON IN
 A PIECE, CUBED

OLIVE OIL FOR FRYING

2–3 TBSP/30–45 ML FLOUR

STOCK OR WATER (SEE METHOD)

1 SMALL GLASS RUM OR COGNAC

SALT AND BLACK PEPPER

FRESH PARSLEY, FINELY
 CHOPPED, AS GARNISH

*First marinate the hare for
2–3 hours with the wine, garlic, 1 onion and herbs, turning
occasionally. Then, over
medium heat, lightly brown the
bacon in a wide, heavy-based
pan large enough to hold all
the ingredients. Add the second
onion (and some oil if the
bacon has not given off enough
fat) and, when it is golden but
not brown, lift the bacon and
onion out of the pan with a
slotted spoon. Remove the meat
from the marinade and pat
dry with paper towels. Make
sure there are at least 2 tbsp
of oil in the pan and then
brown the meat well on all
sides over high heat. Lower the
heat, sprinkle over the flour
and cook until pale golden.
Return the bacon and onion to
(continued on next page)*

19

the pan with the marinade and herbs. The liquid should just cover the meat – if not, add enough stock or water to cover. Heat the rum or cognac in a separate small saucepan, light it with a match and, when the flames have died down, add this to the stew. Bring to a low boil, cover tightly and simmer very gently for about 1½ hours.

When the pieces of hare are tender, remove to a large serving dish and keep warm. Add the liver, finely chopped, and lots of freshly ground black pepper. Boil rapidly for 5–7 minutes, skimming off any surface fat. Turn the heat down very low and stir in the blood until the sauce thickens. (If the blood is not to be used, the sauce should be reduced by boiling until it becomes syrupy.) Season with salt and sieve the sauce, rubbing well to purée the onions, over the hare.

Serve scattered with parsley and surrounded by tiny boiled potatoes or thin flat noodles tossed in good green olive oil.

· TIAN de LAIT RUSTIQUE ·
old-fashioned vanilla cream (6–8)

The lasting richness of a civet is best followed by something simple. This old recipe for vanilla cream was once made with sweetened goat's milk thickened with eggs, but now cow's milk is more common. Serve the pudding with a big dollop of jam in the middle, or rub ¾ lb/375 g fresh fruit – cherries, raspberries, strawberries – through a sieve and spoon the resulting purée around the edges.

---

1 PT/500 ML MILK (GOAT'S MILK
   IF YOU CAN GET IT)
1 STRIP DRIED ORANGE PEEL
1 VANILLA POD
1–2 TBSP/15–30 ML RUM
3 OZ/75 G SUGAR
3 EGGS, BEATEN

· POSSIBLE ADDITION ·
3 PIECES OF CRUSTLESS FRENCH
   BREAD, IN FINE CRUMBS
2 TBSP/30 ML BROWN SUGAR

Preheat the oven to 400°F/ 200°C/gas 6. Heat the milk just to boiling with the orange peel and vanilla pod. Turn down the heat very low and stir in the rum and sugar until the sugar dissolves. Remove from heat and cool for 10 minutes. Take out the vanilla and orange and pour the liquid very slowly into the eggs, stirring continuously. Strain this into 6–8 individual ramekins and stand them

First score the chest-
nuts and either bake
them over a fire
or in a low oven
for about 20
minutes. Peel
them while still
warm and put
them in one layer
in a large heavy-
based frying pan.
Add enough cold water
to come ½ way up the
chestnuts and sprinkle with
several spoonfuls of sugar.
Bring to a very gentle boil
and simmer for 15 minutes
(until the liquid is reduced
and syrupy and the chestnuts
are tender). To serve, squeeze
over lots of lemon juice and
sprinkle with a little caster
sugar.

in a shallow pan of cold
water. Bake until set (about
4–5 minutes). Spoon jam or
puréed fruit on top to serve.

POSSIBLE ADDITION: For a
richer pudding, mix together
the bread and brown sugar
and spread on an oiled baking dish. Bake until caramellized in the preheated oven
and fold into the ramekins of
custard before putting them
in the oven.

* Greedy people
may wish to
serve this
with
cream.

COMPOTE de MARRONS
sugared chestnuts

November is the first
chestnut month in
Provence – baked &
eaten still-hot from
the fire or, as in this
dish, cooked in sugar
for a quick home ver-
sion of marrons glacés.

SWEET CHESTNUTS

SUGAR

LEMON JUICE

ON THE FIRST DAY
OF EVERY YEAR

'IN A TERRACOTTA MARMITE,
GREASED WITH FINELY CHOPPED
PORK FAT, SIMMER AN OLD ROOS-
TER WITH SOME CARROTS &
ONIONS. PERFUME THE BIRD WITH
GARLIC, PARSLEY, THYME & BAY
& BASTE WITH OLIVE OIL FROM
AIX & LATER WITH A GLASS OR
TWO OF BRANDY. WITH THIS
FIRST COCKEREL OF THE NEW
YEAR SERVE A DOZEN PAR-
TRIDGES TO REPRESENT THE 12
MONTHS OF THE YEAR, 30 FRIED
EGGS FOR THE DAYS OF THE
MONTH & 30 PITCH BLACK TRUF-
FLES FOR THE NIGHTS.' (RENÉ
JOUVEAU: 'LA CUISINE PROVEN-
ÇALE DE TRADITION POPULAIRE')

Henceforward
GAUL

When the last jug of buttery cream succumbs to the first jug of olive oil, there lies Provence. The northern border is easy to define; on the march from Elba to Waterloo Napoleon took the northern road, the high road, out of Provence through Sisteron, a town which for centuries has been the gateway to Provence from the county of Dauphiné. The Romans, a few years earlier than the tiny ex-emperor, marched into Provence from the east, over the mountains at La Turbie, 1500 feet above what is now Monte Carlo. Here in 6 BC they erected the massive Tower of Augustus, the Trophy of the Alps – originally 165 feet of monumental stone to commemorate Rome's invincibility. On this were inscribed the words HUC USQE ITALIA ABHINC GALLIA or 'Hitherto Italy Henceforward Gaul'.

Had Rome indeed been invincible, the Tower of Augustus would now be a demarcation point marking the end of Italy & the beginning of Provence, & of Provençal food of course. Unfortunately for the Romans, their power proved less than supreme and the tower served merely as a beacon for dispute; successively neglected, dismantled & generally knocked about for 1700 years until it was finally blown to pieces by the French in 1705, though partially restored since. The border between France & Italy proved as difficult to maintain, & the distinction between Provençal & Italian food even more so, becoming doubly blurred when for 500 years the county of Nice chose to join the house of Savoy in Italy.

*N*ice, restored to France in the 19th century, remains 'Nizza la bella' – home to pasta, pesto & pizza (or pâtes, pistou & pissaladière) – linked more to Genoa than to Marseilles. Provence begins with a France that tastes of Italy & ends where it tastes of Switzerland.

· *ONE DAY IN NICE* ·

*P*etit déjeuner: The catacomb of streets behind the orderly 17th-century houses on the Cours Saleya market are lined with boucheries & boulangeries, pâtisseries, épiceries, charcuteries, fromageries & confiseries. Any space bigger than a cupboard sells food: couscous, pasta, horse meat, wild game (furred & feathered), whole roast suckling pigs. At 8.30 Sunday morning in the city's best bakery, the Four au Bois, half Nice seems to be waiting for André Espuno, who is still putting bread dough into his wood-burning oven at the front of the shop & lifting out (on a long-handled wooden spatula) his famous specialities: 'les mains de Nice', handshaped bread made Italian-style with oil; huge crusty 'deux têtes' & the miniature version 'petites têtes'; fougasses with anchovies, olives, Roquefort or anise; & other Nice breads with walnut or thyme.

*C*asse-croûte: By 10.00 there is a tense crowd around a dark gipsy-like lady next to an oil drum (filled with hot coals to form an impromptu barbecue) in the market. Any uninformed tourists who approach are first deafened – by the woman's punctual half-minute shouts 'saaa KA–LA saaaa KA' – & then puzzled; what are these people waiting for? The answer is a moped that scatters crowds on its lethal way across the market's pedestrian precinct. Stacked precariously on the back of this two-wheeled wasp are wide flying-saucers of the Niçois chickpea crêpe 'socca'. No sooner are these plonked down on the hot oil drum than the gipsy scrapes up the flat blazing-hot corn-yellow pancake in great curls. Money from the crowd flows into the gipsy's pocket as smoothly as olive oil, and satisfied customers disperse clutching waxed-paper cones of the nutty-tasting treat. A new crowd forms to await the next delivery. It is an old Nice routine.

*D*éjeuner: By 11.45 am the market people are dropping their prices & shouting louder, anticipating their lunch. The few remaining tourists who want to eat in the winter sunshine read the chalked menus in the Cours Saleya restaurants, which are not as

cheap as they look. The vast épicerie on the corner of the Place St
François spills the last of its wares on to passing pedestrians; and
Monsieur Ermenegildo Chiodo, who for 30 years has sold the best
porchetta in Nice, pulls down the shop shutters
to leave for the Pizzeria Julian, known to
everyone in the quarter as
Chez Nina.

N ina, born around
the corner from
the restaurant
where

'. . . and when the astronauts landed on the
moon, there arose the sweetest smell on earth, and they
found three Niçois already there, sitting down to
lunch, on pissaladiera, on pissaladiera . . .'

(old Nice folksong)

she is now cook, is a beloved pillar of Old Nice, or as Monsieur
Chiodo calls her, 'une loupe blanche – a fish that is hard to
find but much appreciated when caught'. On Friday
if she is in the mood, Nina cooks a good estocafissado (stockfish stew); but it takes 4–7 days of
soaking to make a dried stockfish even
vaguely edible, so she is as likely to serve
fresh sardines & pissaladière – the
Niçois pizza that is made with onions,
anchovy paste & olives. The
streets rue du Jésus, rue Droite
& rue Ste Réparate were once
filled with women carrying great
iron pots, whose contents perfumed
the old town with the sweet
smelling slow-cooked onions used to
make the

pissaladière. Now pizza rules ... except with Nina, who plays a tape of her friend singing the Pissaladière song to put herself in good spirits (so that ... who knows? – maybe next week the elusive estocafissado will appear as plat du jour?).

· LA MERENDA ·

Nowhere is the heady smell of the Niçois basil & garlic sauce 'pistou' more seductive than at the Giusti family's tiny restaurant La Merenda. By noon each day it is packed with ardent pâtes and pistou eaters. 'Every year someone complains that my pistou is not what it used to be,' said Jean Giusti, 'But this always happens when the basil is still too young – June to September are the best months.'

PÂTES au PISTOU
pasta with basil & garlic sauce (4)

The Giusti family recipe is a loosely guarded secret (and a fairly loose recipe, depending on the basil and garlic season); careful quizzing of regular customers produced this almost identical artery-hardening recipe mixture, not exactly classic, but certainly irresistible (recipe on following page).

*(pâtes au pistou
recipe continued
from previous page.)*

3–4 GARLIC CLOVES,
   PEELED

1 BIG BUNCH FRESH
   BASIL, CLEANED
   & DRIED

4–5 TBSP/60–75 ML
   FRESHLY GRATED
   PARMESAN

3–4 TBSP/45–60 ML
   GOOD OLIVE OIL

12 OZ/350 G THIN
   FLAT PASTA

2 TBSP/30 ML
   CRÈME FRAÎCHE
   (OR DOUBLE/
   HEAVY CREAM)

1 TBSP/15 ML
   BUTTER

SALT & PEPPER

*Pound the garlic
until smooth in a
mortar, then add the
basil leaves and crush
them into the garlic until
they form a paste. Beat the
cheese in with a fork and
begin to add the olive oil drop by
drop, as you would for mayonnaise
or aïoli (page 12). In plenty of
boiling salted water, cook the
pasta until just firm. Drain well
and toss it in a warmed bowl with
cream & butter and plenty of salt
and pepper. Stir in the pistou and
serve immediately.*

** Nice's 'pistou' originated in Genoa as 'pesto'
sauce, made of garlic, butter, cheese, basil and
pine nuts. Deeper into Provence tomatoes take
the place of cheese and butter (see recipe
page 81) to give a cleaner, more fragrant taste.*

½ TSP/2.5 ML NUTMEG
1 TBSP/15 ML THYME,
   FINELY CHOPPED
3 OZ/75 G WHITE
   BREADCRUMBS,
   SOAKED IN MILK
2 TBSP/30 ML CHER-
   VIL, CHOPPED
2 TBSP/30 ML
   CHIVES,
   CHOPPED

· LES SARDINES FARCIES ·
stuffed sardines (4)

Like Nina around the corner, Adrienne Issautier and her husband Jo are well-known characters in old Nice. Together they run the Lou Balico restaurant while Adrienne's sister cooks all the local specialities at their original café on rue Pairolière.

This delightful dish of crispy fresh sardines is delicious with any small fish – mackerel, herring or tiny bream are all very good. It is lifted out of the ordinary by Adrienne's highly decorative method of stuffing the sardines to look like tiny fish sandwiches.

24 SMALL FRESH SARDINES (OR
   OTHER SMALL FISH) EACH
   ABOUT 6–7 IN/15 CM LONG,
   SCALED
FLOUR
SALT & PEPPER
2 LB/1 KG SPINACH OR SWISS
   CHARD TOPS
OLIVE OIL
1 MEDIUM ONION
3 CLOVES GARLIC, FINELY
   CHOPPED

2 EGGS, BEATEN

Preheat the oven to 450°F/ 230°C/gas 8. Cut the heads off the fish, slit them along the belly, remove guts and backbones, leaving tails attached to fish. Open and flatten the fish, sharply twisting the tails all to one side. Sprinkle with a little flour, salt and pepper on the skin side. Wash the spinach very well and cook in a covered saucepan until tender (about 15 minutes). Squeeze out excess moisture and chop spinach finely. Cook the onion and garlic in oil until softened, add spinach, nutmeg and thyme and continue cooking for 5 minutes. Let cool, then mix with squeezed-out breadcrumbs, chervil, chives and eggs. Scoop heaped spoonfuls on to the interior/flesh side of 12 sardines and press the other 12 on top. The tails of each sandwich should be pointing in opposite directions (see drawing). Place the sardines in a well-oiled baking dish, brush surfaces with oil & bake for 10 mins or until fish are brown & tender.

Porc Rôti à la Porchetta
roast pork to taste like porchetta (6)

Thirty-five years ago Ermene-gildo Chiodo arrived in Nice from Piedmont, 11 years old & nothing in his pocket but a recipe for porchetta. He started work in the Charcuterie Saint-François, where, after 14 years, he was helped by his employer to buy out the business. The only competition was from tra-velling porchetta vendors who bicycled from Piedmont over the mountains to Nice. Even now, when the competition is consid-erably more sophisticated, peo-ple come from all over the city to buy their lunchtime por-chetta – stuffed & roasted whole by Monsieur Chiodo every morning at 4.30.

Porchetta, as Monsieur Chiodo makes it, is a whole boned pig stuffed with branches of wild fennel, fennel flowers & its own chopped innards. It is roasted in a blazing hot oven to crisp the skin, then wrapped in cab-bage leaves to stop it hardening. Nothing could taste as good as a thick slice of porchetta still warm from the oven, but this method of roasting a shoulder of pork isn't a bad substitute – for those whose oven can't quite accommodate a whole roast pig.

1 SMALL ONION

OLIVE OIL

2 OZ/50 G WHITE BREAD, CRUMBLED

2–3 SMALL HEADS OF FENNEL WITH LOTS OF FEATHERY LEAVES, FINELY CHOPPED

1 TBSP/15 ML PARSLEY, FINELY CHOPPED

1 TBSP/15 ML THYME, FINELY CHOPPED

½ LB/250 G PORK OFFAL (LIVER, HEART ETC OR JUST LIVER IF PREFERRED), FINELY CHOPPED

SALT & PEPPER

JUICE & GRATED ZEST OF 1 LEMON

3½ LB/1.5 KG BONED SHOULDER OF PORK WITH RIND

½ PINT/300 ML DRY WHITE WINE

2 TBSP/30 ML PASTIS (EG PERNOD, RICARD)

Preheat the oven to 425°F/220°C/ gas 7. Cook the onion in oil until softened. Add the bread, fennel, parsley, thyme & pork offal & cook, stirring often, until the fennel is tender. Sea-son with salt, pepper & lemon.

Score the pork rind deeply. Open up the pocket of the roast & fill with stuffing. Roll pork up & secure with string. (If you have too much stuffing, cook it, covered, in a separate dish for an hour or so in the same oven as the roast.) Rub the joint well with olive oil, coarse salt & black pepper & roast for 20–30 mins, until the skin is golden. Lower the heat to 350°F/180°C/ gas 4 for 1½ hours (raising the heat for the last 15 mins to crisp the skin) until the juice runs amber & not pink. Transfer the pork to a warmed serving plate & remove string. Bring the wine & pastis to a boil in the roasting pan & reduce by half, scraping in all the meat residue. Season with salt & pepper and serve the roast cut in thick slices with a few tbsp of pan juices & a salad of mesclun.

Tourte aux blettes – sweet swiss chard pie: blettes (swiss chard) have always been popular in Nice. Monsieur Chiodo makes a thick, sweet blette pie with crystallized melons & oranges. Down the road at the Four au Bois the same pie is almost flat, stuffed with just a thin layer of blettes, sugar & pine kernels/nuts.

*G*oûter: Tea is in the extravagant Belle Époque confiserie/ salon de thé Maison Auer, established in the rue St-François-de-Paule in 1820. The interior, as flocked and curlicued as one of Jean-Jacques Auer's chocolate boxes, is the high altar of Provençal crystallized fruit, where Russian Grand Dukes used to buy their mistresses lacy confections to while away dull afternoons between assignations. Most crystallized fruit is now produced industrially, but the sugared confiseries of Maison Auer are still proudly 'artisanales' – handmade. It takes a minimum of 60 days to produce a perfect whole crystallized pineapple, and only marginally less time for the kilos of golf ball-sized clementines that simmer in great copper cauldrons at the back of the shop. 88-year-old Henri Auer once said that properly sugared fruit should be 'comme les pneus' – like rubber tyres – fifteen times boiled.

*D*îner: Driving along the palm-tree-lined Promenade des Anglais is like breaking through the hard, sweet crust of some giant wedding cake; miles of increasingly opulent hotels end in the gleaming million-franc – icing-white paint-job of the Hotel Négresco, a monument to Nice's Edwardian glory days. If Old Nice is the dark and chewy fruity centre of the cake, then the Négresco's lascivious pink & green cupola is undoubtedly the sugared bride & groom on top. And Jacques Maximin, the Michelangelo-cum-Napoleon of the haute cuisine world, is the cornerstone that supports the whole baroque edifice.

·TERRINE de BLETTES·
frozen swiss chard
meringue dessert (8)

*Jacques Torres, the Négresco's pastry chef, is 26,
one of the youngest men ever to win the esteemed
title 'Meilleur Ouvrier de France' for his pâtisseries.
He is wildly admiring of Jacques Maximin who, he
says, 'makes the impossible possible'. This beautiful
pale green swiss chard meringue with its smooth
pastis sauce has all the trademarks of both men –
local ingredients (sweetened swiss chard, pine nuts
& pastis are used in many Provençal desserts)
given a flamboyant Négresco twist with the addition of cream & eggs. It is real 'haute cuisine'
which only the most ambitious of cooks should*

attempt, but when successful it is quite sensational.

Inspired by the elaborate creations of nineteenth-century cookbooks (he regrets the loss of that artistry), Jacques Torres believes the key to Provençal cooking is its excellent produce: honeys & lavender flowers , melons, cherries, grapes & fruit eaux-de-vie.

STEP 1 – CRÈME ANGLAISE:

1½ PT/900 ML MILK

1 IN/2.5 CM STRIP ORANGE ZEST

6 OZ/170 G CASTER SUGAR

8 LARGE EGG YOLKS

2 TBSP/30 ML PASTIS

STEP 2:

3 EGG WHITES

5 OZ/150 G CASTER SUGAR

3 SHEETS GELATINE, SOFTENED
   IN A LITTLE COLD WATER &
   HEATED VERY GENTLY IF NECES-
   SARY TO DISSOLVE COMPLETELY

8 FL OZ/240 ML DOUBLE/HEAVY CREAM

8 OZ/250 G TRIMMED SWISS CHARD
   (OR SPINACH) TOPS, COOKED UNTIL
   SOFT, SQUEEZED DRY & PURÉED

WATER (SEE STEP 2)

STEP 3:

12 EGG WHITES

1 LB 5 OZ/600 G SUGAR

6 SHEETS GELATINE, DISSOLVED
   AS ABOVE

1¾ PT/1 LITRE DOUBLE/HEAVY
   CREAM

7 OZ/200 G GREEN SEEDLESS
   GRAPES

7 OZ/200 G PINE KERNELS/NUTS

Step 1: First make the crème anglaise. Heat milk to boiling with orange zest. Meanwhile beat sugar slowly into eggs until mixture forms a ribbon when dropped from beater. Gradually add boiling mik to eggs, beating constantly. Pour into saucepan & heat gently, making sure custard does not boil & stirring constantly with a wooden spoon until mixture just coats spoon in 1 layer. Remove from heat, sieve, place pan in a bowl of iced water, stirring occasionally to prevent skin forming. When cooled a little, beat in pastis. Cover & chill.

Step 2 (meringue using sugar thermometer): Whisk egg whites until very stiff. Heat sugar in 3½ fl oz/100 ml water to 120°C/250°F. Pour this syrup very slowly on to egg whites, beating briskly until amalgamated. Gently fold in dissolved gelatine. Let cool. Beat cream until thickened & fold into swiss chard purée. Fold this into meringue mixture & spread over the base of a large terrine or cake tin. Chill. (Alternative method – meringue without thermometer) Heat together egg whites & sugar, whisking until mixture can be lifted up on whisk. Remove from heat & fold into dissolved gelatine. Proceed as above.

Step 3: Follow Step 2 – either method – for egg whites, sugar & gelatine. Let cool. Whip cream until thick & fold into fruit & nuts. Fold this into meringue mixture & spread over previous layer in terrine. Cover with greaseproof paper & freeze until firm. To serve, briefly dip terrine into hot water, loosen edges with a knife & invert onto a cool plate. Slice and serve with the crème anglaise.

In the foothills of the mountains that appear, like the painted backdrop from an old film, just north-east of Nice, a perpendicular rock shoots dizzyingly up from its valley, its summit supporting the little medieval town of Peillon. From a distance it seems an impossible ascent. Pale mist swirling down from higher snow-covered mountains obscures the base of Peillon's vertical site & not until the final switchback does a link road appear – running along a ridge of pine & olive trees into the town. There, in complete contrast to its dramatic location, is the cosy, pretty Auberge de la Madone – filled with geraniums in summer & in winter with the good smells of Christian Millo's excellent regional cooking.

· TOURTON des PÉNITENTS ·
herb & pine kernel galette (4)

Christian Millo, chef at the Auberge de la Madone, calls this small fat herb galette 'Tourton des Pénitents' because of the pénitents blancs – white-robed pilgrims who used to come on foot to the chapel next to the inn. The eggs in the recipe serve just to bind together the quantities of fresh herbs, cheese & crisp golden pine kernels & the secret is to make sure that no one herb overpowers another. At the Auberge de la Madone Tourton des Pénitents is served as a rather filling but delicious first course on the spring menu.

1½ TBSP/25 ML SPRING ONIONS/ SCALLIONS OR WHITE PART OF A LEEK, FINELY CHOPPED

½ CLOVE GARLIC, CHOPPED

OLIVE OIL

1½ LB/700 G SPINACH OR SWISS CHARD LEAVES

4 TBSP/60 ML PINE KERNELS/NUTS

4 TBSP/6 ML CHIVES, FINELY CHOPPED

1 TBSP/15 ML (APPROX) EACH, FINELY CHOPPED OF:

FRESH MINT (OR BASIL IN SEASON)

SAVORY

THYME

CHERVIL

3 LARGE EGGS

3 TBSP/45 ML FRESH DOUBLE/ HEAVY CREAM (CRÈME FRAÎCHE FOR PREFERENCE)

5 OZ/125 G GRUYÈRE, GRATED

SALT & PEPPER

Cook the spring onions or leek & garlic in oil until softened. Blanch the spinach or swiss chard briefly, squeeze out the moisture very well & chop finely. Mix together all the ingredients except eggs, cream & cheese & pour into a large well-oiled frying pan. Cook for about 5 mins over high heat until herbs have softened but are still green, remove from heat and drain off any liquid. Beat together the eggs, cream & cheese & pour into the herb mixture, mixing well. Return mixture to stove & continue cooking over a medium heat, pressing it into a round thick shape with a wooden spoon.

After about 10–15 mins, when one side has browned well, cover the pan with a dish, tip the tourton onto it, then slide it, top side down, back into the pan. Cook until golden & serve, still sizzling, on a very hot plate with a few tablespoons of tomato coulis.

· COULIS de TOMATES ·
good tomato purée

OLIVE OIL

2½ LB/1 KG VERY RIPE TOMATOES, DICED

1 ONION, FINELY CHOPPED

1 TSP/5 ML SUGAR

BOUQUET GARNI OF THYME, BAY & ROSEMARY

SALT & PEPPER

Heat 2 tbsp/30 ml of oil & cook everything except salt & pepper for 15–20 minutes. Sieve & cook uncovered for 30–40 minutes. Season with salt & pepper & store, covered with a layer of olive oil, in small jars in the refrigerator.

· CONFITURE d'OIGNONS ·
onion chutney

Around the Monte Carlo area there is an old recipe for tiny sweet & sour onions – oignons à la monégasque – that is surely the grandfather of this modern spicy onion chutney. This is excellent with the Caillettes on page 125 & Christian Millo serves a similar preserve with a slab of his luscious Terrine à l'Ancienne. At the Auberge Provençale in Eygalières it is served simply with scrubbed pink radishes & crusty bread.

3 LB/1.5 KG SMALL ONIONS, SLICED LENGTHWISE FINELY

1 LB/500 G COOKING APPLES, PEELED, CORED & DICED

JUICE & HALF GRATED ZEST OF 1 LEMON

½ PT/300 ML WATER

⅔ PT /350 ML SHERRY OR WHITE WINE VINEGAR

¾ LB/350 G WHITE SUGAR

4 OZ/100 G GOOD TOMATO COULIS

4 TBSP/60 ML STRONG-TASTING FLOWER HONEY (ACACIA, LAVENDER ETC)

1 TSP/5 ML SYRUP FROM PRESERVED GINGER (OPTIONAL – OR USE A LITTLE EXTRA HONEY)

½ TSP/2.5 ML SALT

1 TSP/5 ML CINNAMON

1 TSP/5 ML CAYENNE PEPPER

Place the onions, apples, lemon and water in a large stainless steel or aluminium saucepan & simmer for 20 mins. Add half the vinegar, cover & simmer over low heat until the onions are very tender. Add the sugar dissolved in remaining vinegar, tomato coulis, honey, ginger syrup (if used), salt, cinnamon & cayenne pepper and continue cooking for another 20 minutes or until thick and syrupy. Leave to stand for 10 mins and remove any scum that forms on top. Pour the still warm chutney into clean warm jars and seal well.

Not far north of Peillon is Lucéram, whose close proximity to Provence's border with Italy is much in evidence: at least half the town's 550 residents appear to speak Piedmontese, the local Italian dialect. One cold February day, while new snow clouds rolled in behind the fifteenth-century church tower, Lucéram's mayor, his two guests, the entire staff of the Hotel Méditerranée, and three of the hotel's ancient residents sat in the restaurant discussing, in a curious linguistic mixture of Provençal and Italian, the past and present of the local gastronomy. Monsieur le Maire could just be heard above the squawks of the parrot in the window and the Gitane roar of Joséphine, the 69-year-old grande dame of the Méditerranée.

· LA SOUPE de COURGE ·
pumpkin soup (6)

Giant orange pumpkins, called, perhaps misleadingly for a foreigner, 'courges' in Provence, are a speciality in the Lucéram region. They're used as pizza topping when tomatoes are not in season, and in soups to make a French version of minestrone, or this creamy-sweet orange bisque. Both soups are particularly good served in the scooped-out shell of the pumpkin.

2 LB/1 KG PUMPKIN FLESH, DICED

½ LB/250 G FLOURY POTATOES, PEELED AND DICED

3 LEEKS, TRIMMED AND FINELY CHOPPED

1 CLOVE GARLIC, CRUSHED

2 TBSP/30 ML FRESH MARJORAM, FINELY CHOPPED

½ TSP/2.5 ML NUTMEG

3½ PT/2 LITRE BOUILLON (OR WATER)

SALT AND PEPPER

2 OZ/50 G RICE

4 OZ/100 G GRUYÈRE, GRATED

3 HARD-BOILED EGGS, CHOPPED

Place all ingredients except eggs, cheese & rice into a deep saucepan. Bring to a boil & then simmer for 30 mins. Purée, add salt & pepper & bring back to a low boil. Add rice & continue simmering for about 20 mins until tender. Pour soup into the hollowed-out pumpkin & garnish with grated cheese and chopped egg.

• LA SOUPE aux CHÂTAIGNES •
chestnut soup (4)

Fifty years ago, before the ski industry brought a degree of prosperity to the region, the Lucéram villagers were considered rich because soup was not their main course but only an entrée. Their neighbours to the north wintered on a diet of polenta (with the occasional game bird thrown in) and chestnuts. This surprisingly elegant soup dates from those pre-tourism times.

1½ LB/700 G CHESTNUTS (FRESH OR DRIED)

RED WINE

3 LEEKS, FINELY CHOPPED

1½ PT/1 LITRE GOOD BOUILLON

SALT & PEPPER

1 HEAPED COFFEE CUP COOKED RICE

1 TBSP/15 ML PARSLEY OR CHERVIL, CHOPPED

To peel chestnuts (if you are using fresh ones) cut a cross on the side of each nut, then boil them in water for several minutes. When cool enough to handle, remove shells and inner skins. Soak chestnuts in red wine for 2 hours. Drain nuts and put in a large saucepan with the leeks, bouillon & salt. Cover, bring to the boil, then simmer for 45 minutes, or until the nuts are tender.

Remove several large chestnuts, purée the soup and reheat with the cooked rice. Season to taste and serve with the whole chestnuts and some chervil on top. For a richer soup you may wish to swirl in some fromage frais (see recipe page 50), which makes a lovely contrast to the bland sweetness of the chestnuts.

la petite soupe 6 Frs le paquet

· CAILLE à la POLENTE ·
polenta with quail sauce (4)

When asked how & when to serve this dish, Joséphine let out a gusty wheeze, "But in the winter of course – polenta hot & steaming on the bottom so the poor little birds can keep their feet warm!"

She makes enough polenta to fill a huge pot – this smaller quantity is more manageable.

POLENTA:

1½ PT/1 LITRE BOUILLON, PREFERABLY HOMEMADE

1 TBSP/15 ML CHOPPED FRESH PARSLEY

1 TBSP/15 ML CHOPPED FRESH THYME

8 OZ/225 G COARSE GRAINED POLENTA

1 TBSP/15 ML OLIVE OIL

· QUAIL ·

8 QUAIL (OR 4 POUSSINS, PIGEONS, WOODCOCKS OR ROCK

CORNISH GAME HENS) WITH
  GIBLETS

OLIVE OIL

COARSE SALT

WHITES OF 2 LEEKS, THINLY
  SLICED

BRANCH OF THYME PER BIRD

8 THIN SHEETS OF LARDING FAT
  OR

8 THIN SLICES UNSMOKED BACON

2 CLOVES GARLIC, FINELY
  CHOPPED

1 ONION, FINELY CHOPPED

1 LARGE RIPE TOMATO, PEELED,
  SEEDED & CHOPPED

10 FL OZ/300 ML CHICKEN OR
  BEEF STOCK

5 FL OZ/150 ML RED WINE

SALT & PEPPER

• TO DECORATE •

A LITTLE JUICE & 2 TBSP/30 ML
  FINELY SHREDDED ZEST
  OF LEMON

CHOPPED FRESH CHERVIL

First make the polenta: put the bouillon in a big saucepan & bring to a low boil. Pour in the polenta in a slow steady stream, thin enough to see the individual grains, stirring constantly with a stout wooden spoon. Add 1 tbsp/15 ml olive oil & the herbs, & continue stirring until the polenta begins to leave the sides of the pan. Pour the polenta into a greased rectangular cake tin & leave to cool.

Preheat the oven to 200°C/400°F/gas 6. Remove the giblets from the birds & reserve. Rub the inside of the birds with olive oil & coarse salt & stuff them with the leek & thyme. Wrap birds in larding fat or bacon, truss them & roast in a flameproof dish for 35–45 minutes, depending on size, or until juices run clear yellow. Cut off trussing strings & keep birds warm. Reset oven to 230°C/450°F/gas 8. Chop the giblets finely & add to the roasting pan with the garlic & onion. Cook gently over low flame for a couple of minutes. Add the tomato, chicken stock & wine & boil rapidly, scraping the pan well, until the juice has reduced by about half. Season with salt & pepper. For a more elegant dish you may wish to sieve the sauce at this point. Otherwise remove polenta from its dish & cut it into ½ in/12 mm slices. Lay them in one overlapping layer in an oiled casserole & arrange the birds on top. Cover with foil & heat through in the oven. To serve, squeeze a little lemon juice over the top & decorate with zest & chervil.

Grand-père's polenta treat

When Joséphine's grandfather was alive he solved the problem of leftover polenta – it was cut into little rounds about the thickness of a slice of bread. On top went a smear of sharp mustard, then a wedge of Gruyère & a couple of the tiny strawberry-sweet Provençal tomatoes, cut in half. The polenta was sizzled quickly in a little olive oil until the cheese began to run and then sprinkled with salt and fresh black pepper.

· CHÂTEAU ARNOUX ·

*P*ierre Gleize would still be making sugared violets in Apt
if he hadn't stopped one day at an 18th-century posthouse
in Château Arnoux. Inside he found a new career as chef &
the future Madame Gleize, whose family had run the inn for
generations.

*C*hâteau Arnoux is close to Provence's north-east border, a
region that Provençal author Jean Giono called a 'land of
no excesses', & that Pierre Gleize compares to the Scottish
highlands. 'But we have everything here, save good beef &
good cream,' he says, 'and what's more – we have sunshine!'
From nearby Sisteron comes the lamb – not fattened on grass
but on wild rosemary & thyme – to make the Gleize family's
jambon cru d'agneau, cured & sliced like Parma ham. From
their gardens come sweet hyssop for roast rabbit, young
spring vegetables, fragile courgette flowers, & lavender honey
to baste a roast duckling. This is also one of the few starred
Michelin restaurants to serve the old-fashioned local dishes
tarte aux potirons (pumpkin pie) and pâte de coings (a
sweetmeat of sugared quince paste).

· CANETON au MIEL ·
de LAVANDE et au CITRON
duckling in lemon
& lavender honey sauce (6)

In spring Haute Provence is
covered in fruit tree blossoms.
And when the blossoms fall, the
lavender begins – miles of purple, striped with bleached
earth. People in Provence have
always made nougat & sweetened cheese with honey from
these lavender fields, but to use
it in meat & poultry dishes is a
recent development; surprisingly, considering Provence's
long Arab history.

3 DUCKLINGS (WITH GIBLETS, IF
   POSSIBLE) OF ABOUT 3 LB/1.4 KG,
   PLUCKED & CLEANED

PEPPER & SALT

BUTTER OR OLIVE OIL FOR FRYING

· STOCK ·

DUCKLING GIBLETS*

BUTTER FOR FRYING

2 CARROTS, CHOPPED

1 ONION, CHOPPED

1 SPRIG THYME

½ BAY LEAF

9 FL OZ/275 ML WHITE WINE

* (IF YOU CAN'T FIND DUCKLING
WITH GIBLETS TO MAKE THIS
STOCK, SUBSTITUTE 7 FL OZ/200 ML
GOOD CHICKEN STOCK INSTEAD)

· SAUCE ·

3½ FL OZ/90 ML WINE VINEGAR

2 TSP/10 ML LAVENDER HONEY

4 TBSP/60 ML LEMON JUICE

7 OZ/200 ML STOCK (SEE ABOVE)

2 OZ/50 G BUTTER

SALT & PEPPER

Preheat the oven to 425°F/ 220°C/gas 7. First prepare the ducklings: remove excess fat from within body cavity, cut off lower wings & keep them with the giblets to make stock. Season the ducklings inside & out with salt & pepper & tie legs & wings to the body to ensure even cooking. To make the stock, cook the giblets & wing tips in a little butter and add the vegetables and herbs. Stir well, pour in the wine and enough cold water to cover. Let this simmer while you cook the ducklings: brown them on all sides in butter and then roast in a hot oven for about 20 minutes, or until cooked to taste, basting often. When done, remove from the oven and keep warm. Deglaze the roasting pan with vinegar, & when this is reduced to just a thick syrup, add the honey, lemon juice and stock (first sieved). Let this bubble until thickened, stir in the butter

and season with salt and pepper. Slice the duckling breast, fan it out on a warmed serving plate, cut off the legs and grill briefly on both sides. Serve moistened with the honey and lemon sauce.

Fleurs de Courgettes Farcies Sauce Pomme d'Amour

stuffed courgette/zucchini flowers in tomato coulis (6)

The Gleize family present only the season's best ingredients. One day in early spring Madame Gleize apologized for the absence of their usual superb stuffed courgette flowers. 'But you know, the asparagus is very good & tender. And today is the first Sunday of the morel season. Everyone is out hunting like mad; so tomorrow...'

• SAUCE •

18 OZ/500 G FIRM RIPE TOMATOES, PEELED & SEEDED

GRATED ZEST (BUT NO WHITE PITH) OF 1 LEMON

3–4 BASIL LEAVES, FINELY CHOPPED

1 TBSP/15 ML PARSLEY, FINELY CHOPPED

1 TBSP/15 ML CHERVIL, FINELY CHOPPED

PINCH OF POWDERED CORIANDER

1 GARLIC CLOVE, PEELED & CRUSHED

4 FL OZ/100 ML OLIVE OIL

SALT & PEPPER

• STUFFING •

3 MEDIUM COURGETTES, FINELY CHOPPED (A BLENDER WORKS)

6 TBSP/90 ML OLIVE OIL

6 FRESH BASIL LEAVES, IN THIN STRIPS

6 FRESH MINT LEAVES, CHOPPED

HANDFUL FRESH PARSLEY, FINELY CHOPPED

2 SMALL GARLIC CLOVES, PEELED & FINELY CHOPPED

SALT & PEPPER

GENEROUS HANDFUL FINE STALE BREADCRUMBS

1 EGG, BEATEN

9 FL OZ/250 ML CHICKEN STOCK

18 LARGE COURGETTE FLOWERS (PICKED JUST BEFORE YOU NEED TO USE THEM IF POSSIBLE)

Prepare sauce at least 12 hours before: crush tomatoes with a fork, & beat in the lemon zest, herbs, coriander, garlic & olive oil. Season well with salt and pepper. Do not refrigerate. To make the stuffing, cook the courgettes in 2 tbsp/30 ml of olive oil. When softened, remove from heat & mix with basil, mint, parsley, garlic, salt and pepper. Allow to cool & add the breadcrumbs and beaten egg. Remove pistils from flowers, then put a spoonful of the stuffing into each flower, tuck in the ends & lay the flowers side by side in an ovenproof dish. Pour over the stock & remaining olive oil, cover with foil & bake for 15 minutes in an oven preheated to 350°F/180°C/gas 4. To serve, spoon a little tomato coulis onto each plate & place 3 flowers on top.

· *FAYENCE* ·

*I*n the cosy garlic-hung Restaurant France, they serve giant platters of crisp fresh crudités, plump chickens roasted with pine kernels and herbs, and light, eggy fruit tarts, all simple and good.

· POULET aux PIGNONS ·
roast chicken
with pine kernels/nuts (4)

This is less a recipe than a taste of winter in Provence to transform even the most tasteless of chickens.

3 LB/1.5 KG ROASTING CHICKEN

1 LEMON

4–6 TBSP/60–90 ML CHOPPED
    FRESH HERBS SUCH AS THYME,
    MARJORAM, SAVORY

OLIVE OIL

SALT & FRESHLY GROUND PEPPER

4–6 TBSP/50–90 ML PINE
    KERNELS/NUTS

WHITE WINE (OPTIONAL)

CHOPPED FRESH CHERVIL TO
    DECORATE

Preheat the oven to 400°F/ 200°C/gas 6. Wipe inside of chicken with a damp cloth and pat dry. Squeeze the lemon halves into the chicken and place them in the breast cavity with 2 tbsp/30 ml of chopped herbs. Brush the chicken with olive oil, sprinkle with pepper and remaining herbs, except chervil, and roast the chicken for 1 hour 20 minutes breast side down, then 20 minutes each breast side up, basting occasionally after the first 20 minutes. Remove to a warm serving dish and add pine kernels to roasting pan. Cook over a high heat, scraping the pan well with a spatula, until the nuts are toasted brown. You may want to pour in a glass of the wine you're drinking as well, in which case reduce it by half and then pour the pine kernels and pan juices over the chicken. Decorate with chervil and serve.

· BARGEMON ·

In the plane tree-lined town of Bargemon, the cooks like to serve fresh basil sauce with fried chicken and rabbit all year round. Even in Provence there is no winter supply of this peppery herb, so it is picked in large bunches in the summer and puréed with good olive oil. Stored in tightly-sealed jars in the refrigerator, it will add a taste of summer to your cooking all through the cold months.

· POULET FARCI au BASILIC ·
chicken stuffed with basil (4)

This is just one of many ways to use the infinitely versatile fresh basil purée. The chicken breasts are delicious simply stuffed with this and grilled, but for a more elaborate and richer dish serve them with this creamy leek and basil sauce.

4 CHICKEN BREASTS

5 TBSP/75 ML BASIL PURÉE

SALT & FRESHLY GROUND BLACK
   PEPPER

1 LEEK, FINELY SLICED

¾ PT/400 ML FROMAGE FRAIS
   (PAGE 50) OR BOUGHT CREAM
   CHEESE (THE LOW-FAT, SEMI-
   LIQUID KIND) OR SINGLE
   CREAM

Carefully lift the skin off each piece of chicken, leaving it attached at one end. Cut a slit in the centre of each breast and stuff with 1 tbsp of basil purée. Cover again with the skin, sprinkle with salt and pepper and grill for 15–20 minutes each side, or until the juice from the thickest part runs clear. Meanwhile, make the sauce: in a non-stick pan, cook the leek until tender in a little of the basil purée oil. Add the fromage frais and reduce by about half over a very gentle heat. At the last minute stir in 1 tbsp/15 ml of basil purée, pour the sauce over the grilled chicken and serve.

· PURÉE de BASILIC ·
basil purée

FRESH BASIL LEAVES

OLIVE OIL

Chop finely or pound the basil leaves to a purée in a mortar. Add the olive oil, allowing about 1 tbsp/15 ml for every ten leaves. Pack in small jars with a little more oil on top to cover, and seal well.

*T*he old olive oil mill at the base of hilltop Opio near Grasse has been in the Michel family for seven generations & the remains of a mill dating back as far as the fifteenth century can still be seen. From mid-November until March,

depending on the season, two sets of mill equipment, one modern & the other more antiquated, grind tiny ripe Niçois olives into rich green olive oil, to be sold in gleaming tins in the mill store.

Salade de Tomates à l'Orange
tomato & orange salad (4)

Don't be put off by the quantity of salt and vinegar specified in this tart tomato salad, but do drain the tomatoes well after marinating. And, as in all dishes where olive oil is an important seasoning, use the best you can afford – a little goes a long way.

4 LARGE OR 6–8 SMALLER JUICY TOMATOES, EACH CUT IN 8

1 TBSP/15 ML FINE SALT

GROUND BLACK PEPPER

4 TBSP/60 ML TARRAGON WINE VINEGAR

JUICE AND FINELY SHREDDED ZEST OF 1 SMALL ORANGE

4 TBSP/60 ML OLIVE OIL

Place the tomatoes in a bowl and mix well with the salt, pepper, vinegar, orange juice and 2 tbsp/30 ml olive oil. Leave in a cool place for 2–3 hours. Just before serving remove the tomatoes, drain very well and toss in 2 tbsp/30 ml fresh oil. Scatter the shredded zest over the top & serve.

·La Daurade du Pêcheur·
fisherman's baked bream (4)

The olive oil in this dish is used to add its own unctuous peppery taste and

to keep the sometimes dry flesh of the bream moist.

slices and rub with coarse sea salt and freshly ground pepper. Lay the vegetables in a greased oval baking dish with the fish on top, drizzle the cooking juices over the top and bake for about 20 minutes. Just before serving, spoon a little more olive oil over the fish and take to the table in its dish.

---

4 SPRING ONIONS/SCALLIONS, SPLIT IN HALF LENGTHWISE

2 SMALL HEADS FENNEL (WITH LEAFY TOPS), FINELY SHREDDED

2 OZ/50 G GOOD MUSHROOMS, SLICED FINELY

5 TBSP/75 ML OLIVE OIL

1 TOMATO, PEELED, DE-SEEDED & SLICED

GENEROUS PINCH OF SAFFRON THREADS OR POWDER

1 LARGE WINEGLASS DRY WHITE WINE

1½ LB/700 G BREAM

COARSE SEA SALT & FRESHLY GROUND BLACK PEPPER

Preheat oven to 350°F/180°C/ gas 4. In a large frying pan gently cook the onion, fennel and mushrooms in 2 tbsp oil until softened. Add the tomatoes and saffron, cook for 5 minutes and add the wine. Continue cooking for several minutes. Meanwhile slash the fish to the bone in 3 diagonal

· AURIBEAU ·

Here in the countryside north of Cannes, where the villas are piled on top of each other like slabs of paving stones up the hills, the little village of Auribeau and its Auberge Nossi Be sit serenely above them all.

· LES GOUJONETTES de SOLE · aux PISTILS de SAFRAN et son FLAN de MOULES au CERFEUIL

fillets of sole in saffron with mussel and chervil baked custard (6)

Young Monsieur Retore, owner and chef at the Nossi Be, serves his delicate mussel custard as a centrepiece to twists of sole in a subtle, almost sweet, yellow saffron sauce. The custard is good enough to make on its own with a crisp salad, or maybe with toast as a first course.

· FOR THE MUSSELS ·

2 PT/1 LITRE SMALL FRESH
  MUSSELS (FOR PREFERENCE
  THE TINY SWEET ONES CALLED
  BOUCHOTS)
2 EGGS
½/250 ML DOUBLE/HEAVY CREAM
CHERVIL
SALT & PEPPER

· FOR THE SOLE ·

2 TBSP/30 ML SHALLOTS, FINELY
  CHOPPED
12 FILLETS OF SOLE
½ PT/250 ML DRY WHITE WINE
SALT & BLACK PEPPER
4 OZ/100 G BUTTER, CUT IN SMALL
  PIECES
1 GENEROUS PINCH SAFFRON
  THREADS OR POWDER
½ PT/250 ML DOUBLE/HEAVY
  CREAM, LIGHTLY BEATEN
TOMATOES (PREFERABLY TINY
  SWEET CHERRY TOMATOES)
  FOR DECORATION

Preheat oven to 350°F/180°C/ gas 4. Clean the mussels: wash them under cold running water and scrape any weed and dirt off with a knife. Discard any that are not firmly closed or that seem unreasonably heavy. Put them in a large pot, cover tightly and cook over a high heat, shaking the pot vigorously several times, until the mussels have just opened (5–7 minutes). Remove them from their shells and divide them between 6 buttered ramekins. Beat together the (continued on next page) eggs, cream and chervil, season with salt and pepper and pour into the ramekins. Cover with buttered paper and cook in a bain-marie for about 20 minutes.

Meanwhile prepare the sole: scatter a buttered baking dish with the chopped shallots. Lay the fillets of sole on top and moisten with the wine and a few tablespoons of cold water. Sprinkle with salt and black pepper and cover the dish with a piece of buttered paper. When the flans have set, remove from oven and leave to stand in a warm place. Turn the oven up to 425°F/220°C/gas 7 and bake the sole for about 15 minutes. Remove the fish and keep warm. Reduce the cooking juices by half over a high heat, little by little adding the butter and saffron. When reduced, stir in the cream and remove from heat. Gently shake the mussel custards from their dishes into the centre of each plate. Pour the sauce round each custard, place the fillets on top and decorate with small pieces of fresh tomato or sprigs of fresh chervil.

*T*he face of Madame Agnèse, whose family has been in the cheese business since 1914, lights up at the thought of the festival in Cannes. 'All the big names will be there,' she says with excitement. She is not referring to the Cannes Film Festival, of course, but to the slightly less famous Cannes cheese festival in May. Even more enthusiasts than usual will pack her tiny, immaculate shop on the rue d'Antibes, to choose from the shelves of strangely shaped and curiously textured little goats' cheeses that rest on their beds of straw and leaves.

· *OMELETTE au BROCCIO* ·
sweet goat's cheese omelette with fresh mint (2)

This sweet omelette has a rich, melting texture and the tang of fresh mint. It is an ideal way of using the mild and creamy Corsican goat (and ewe) cheese Broccio, or the stronger tasting Brin d'Amour with its covering of wild herbs that smell of mint and new-mown hay.

½ OZ/15 G UNSALTED BUTTER

3 FRESH MINT LEAVES, CUT IN THIN
    STRIPS

3 EGGS, LIGHTLY BEATEN WITH
    2 TSP/10 ML SUGAR

3 TBSP/45 ML MILD GOAT CHEESE
    (FRESH CORSICAN FOR
    PREFERENCE), DICED

1 TBSP/15 ML DOUBLE/HEAVY CREAM

SUGAR FOR SPRINKLING

2 MINT LEAVES FOR DECORATION

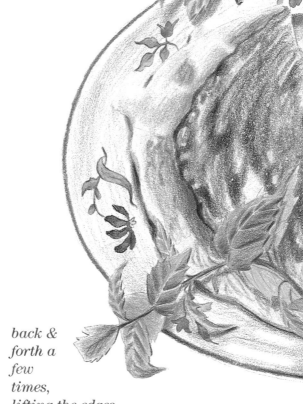

Heat a 10 in/25 cm omelette pan. Melt the butter with the strips of mint over a high heat. When the bubbles start to die down, add the eggs, followed immediately by the cheese and the cream spooned over the top. Tip the pan back & forth a few times, lifting the edges of the omelette with a spatula to let the liquid egg run underneath.

The instant the surface of the omelette is no longer runny but is still loose and creamy, fold it in three lengthwise by flipping the

(continued on next page)

edges to the middle and slide on to a very hot plate. Sprinkle sugar over the top, decorate with mint leaves and serve immediately.

· FROMAGE FRAIS ·
à la CIBOULETTE
homemade fresh cheese with chives (1 lb/500 g)

In Provence every cheese shop worthy of its whey has an earthenware bowl (or several) with a big wooden spoon stuck in its mound of soft, fresh cheese. Some of this 'fromage frais' is plain, to be eaten with crème fraîche and honey or homemade jam, some is scented with fresh herbs, the most popular on the Côte d'Azur being a mixture of chives and chervil. If you are lucky, the fresh cheese will be made from goat's milk, as it is at the Maison Agnèse. This is a simple home version using full cream cow's milk.

3 PT/1.5 LITRES FULL CREAM MILK

1 PT/500 ML DOUBLE/HEAVY CREAM

2 SCANT TSP/10 ML LIQUID RENNET

1 TSP/5 ML SALT

SEVERAL GRINDS BLACK PEPPER

2 TBSP/30 ML FRESH CHIVES, ROUGHLY CHOPPED (AND A FEW WHOLE PURPLE FLOWERS IF YOU HAVE THEM)

2 TBSP/30 ML FRESH CHERVIL OR PARSLEY, ROUGHLY CHOPPED (PLUS MORE TO DECORATE IF YOU HAVE NO CHIVE FLOWERS)

OR

2 TBSP OF THE FRESH BASIL SAUCE ON PAGE 44

1 LARGE OPEN-WEAVE BASKET, OR SEVERAL SMALL ONES

PIECE OF MUSLIN OR CHEESE-CLOTH, APPROX 1 YD/METRE

Heat the milk and cream in a large pan until lukewarm. Stir the rennet into the mixture very thoroughly. Remove the pan from heat, cover with a clean cloth and let stand until the curd is fairly solid (3–5 hours). Place the curd in a sieve lined with a double thickness of damp muslin and leave to drain over a deep bowl for about 1½ hours in a cool place. Remove the cheese and gently work in the

herbs into the top. Serve instead of mayonnaise with a bowl of crudités & crusty bread. (The cheese will keep for about 3 days in a cold place. Alternatively, if you wish to use the cheese to thicken sauces, or with honey and cream, omit the herbs, salt and pepper.)

At the delightful Auberge Jarrière in Biot they serve the fromage frais separately, surrounded by little bowls of sugar, honey and chopped fresh herbs – a sort of do-it-yourself version of this recipe.

> *Banons* are small goat's cheeses, wrapped in eau-de-vie-soaked chestnut leaves, tied with raffia. *Boutons de culotte*, the tiny mouthful-sized 'Trouser button' goat's cheeses, have hollow straws through the middle to age them quickly. *Roquefort* is a prized ewe's milk cheese often used in Provençal pasta sauces & winter salads.

salt, pepper and herbs, leaving the chive flowers and a few chopped herbs for decoration later. Line the basket with muslin and press the cheese firmly into it. Leave to drain again for 24 hours – the longer you leave it the firmer it will set. Turn out on to a plate and press the chive flowers and more chopped

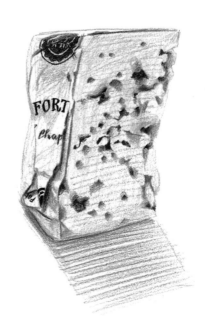

A SHOPPING DAY *IN NICE*

*BLACK NIÇOIS OLIVES & OLIVE
OIL FROM ALZIARI • CLEMENTINE
JAM, BRANDIED CHERRIES &
GLACÉ PINEAPPLE FROM AUER •
FRESH NIÇOIS RAVIOLI FROM
MAISON QUIRINO • TRULLES
(NIÇOIS BLACK PUDDING MADE
WITH SWISS CHARD) FROM AU
JAMBON DE YORK • HOT SOCCA
(TERESA'S), FRESH HERBS &
FLOWERS FROM THE SATURDAY
MARKET (FARMERS' DAY) IN THE
COURS SALEYA • A BOTTLE OF
NICE'S RARE BELLET WINE
(CHÂTEAU DE BELLET 1982) •*

Between two
CITIES

Marseilles is
not unlike the favourite shellfish – the sea-urchin – of
its citizens: an unprepossessing exterior masking a
strong, addictive taste of the sea. It is not a tourists' city,
although it is perhaps, to make a fine distinction, one for tra-
vellers. It is, at all odds, the oldest city in France, yet there
are few antiquities, few 'sights' for the avid ruin seeker. And
more than any other place in Provence, it pays here to speak
the language. Without it, Marseilles' rich street life is not tan-
talizing but threatening; the rowdy fishwives' jokes on the
Quai des Belges seem more cruel than amusing & the authen-
ticity of two identical cafés in the old port, both claiming 'La
vraie Bouillabaisse', is not apparent until too late. With even
a few words of encouragement, any Marseillais – from taxi-
driver to journalist – will tell you the three best places to try
the famous fish soup. Not surprisingly, none of these three
receive Michelin stars. In spite of the smart boutiques along
the rue de Rome & the burgeoning antique shops off the Place
Thiars, the real heart of Marseilles remains working class.

The same cannot be said of Aix-en-Provence, one of
France's most elegant & aristocratic small cities. Inextric-
ably linked by commerce with Marseilles, culturally it is
poles apart. While the Cours Mirabeau in Aix, called the most
beautiful main street in the world, is a broad, tree-lined
boulevard of bookshops, terrace cafés & eighteenth-century
mansions, Marseilles' equivelant street, the Canebière, with

its cut-price stores & cafeterias, binds the tragic & sinister Arab quarter in the west with the east-side market streets.

*A*ix-en-Provence is a city of fountains. The sound of water is inescapable in the old quarter, where a maze of restored, boutique-lined streets open on to cobbled squares & spouting dolphins. The Vieux Port of Marseilles was once a maze as well, so full of pimps & prostitutes, Resistance heroes & pickpockets & Foreign Legionnaires & sailors, that in 1943 the Germans, under the pretext that the area was an uncontrollable health hazard (to themselves, presumably), evicted the 40,000 residents & blew it up. But north of the rue Caisserie, the old town – 'the Panier' or bread basket, as it is known affectionately in Marseilles – still survives. Houses are linked by washing lines & in streets noisy with scruffy children & gossiping women, anonymous doorways lead to tiny restaurants where, for those not too frightened to risk the occasional minor disaster, one can usually eat cheaply & well.

*E*ating well in Aix-en-Provence is not as easy as it should be. But the pastry-shops are indisputably superb & the cafés are Aix's bloodstream. Sit in faded Empire elegance in the famous Deux Garçons café & watch the parade of language students from the university, judges, town ladies whose hairstyles match their poodles, & in July visitors to the annual music festival. 'Oh we never go to the the two Gs,' said one client of another bar, 'That's for the snobs with their copies of the Le Monde.'

*M*arseilles is more famous for a fictional bar. In the 1930s Marcel Pagnol became a national hero because of his trilogy of plays (later films) 'Marius', 'Fanny' & 'César' that span 30 years in the life of César, owner of a bar on Marseilles' Vieux Port, & his sometimes erring family and friends. 'Never will I leave my bar,' César says; 'I want to die while mixing a Picon-citron drink, and, if such a thing is allowed, to be buried here under the counter.'

*C*esar's pride in his bar was rooted in a time when Marseilles' bars were social clubs for temporarily homeless men. In the middle ages there was a constant flow of trade between Italy & Marseilles; Italian sailors & fishermen, waiting for the next ship, rented minuscule rooms in the alleys of the port. But they lived in the bars, known as 'cantines', below these rooms. There, for a few francs, they could eat good sausage & cheese, drink, gossip & fight until it was time to sleep.

And one day, when the biggest fish seemed always the one nearest Marseilles, or when the next ship took too long to sail, these Pisans, Genoans & Neapolitans married local girls & made their new city home.

Immigration of both Italian men & women increased during Napoleon III's time until, for every four students in Marseilles, two were Italian. France's empire needed workers, & Marseilles was enjoying its greatest commercial boom. Genoese women were valued because they could carry loads of fish & vegetables in baskets on their heads, while women from Naples moved into tiny shops to sell a few essentials & serve simple dishes. Good cooks became known all over the old port & their modern grand-daughters haven't lost respect for their Italian origins. Even today, homes in Marseilles serve Neapolitan recipes more scrupulously authentic than those in Naples. 'But our families have no nostalgia for Italy – Marseilles is home,' said Anne Sportiello, a fifth-generation French-Italian, & curator of the museum of old Marseilles. 'The Italians integrated well here because it was like their old villages: close to their fishing boats, with shops on every corner & sunny squares for the children. Even the food was similar, simple & tasty with a base of cereals, fish, vegetables & herbs.'

It takes about 20 minutes to travel between Aix-en-Provence & Marseilles but more than just a few miles of road separate the two. Visitors to Aix are constantly reminded of her glorious past – as Roman spa from 123 BC, as capital of Provence from the twelfth to the eighteenth century – and of her brilliant present status as university town & centre for the arts. And Marseilles? Two stories capture perhaps a little of this tough old city's independent spirit. One day an old Marseillais in the Panier, a passionate player of Pétanque (bowls), was tired of waiting for the mistral to stop blowing. He filled his living room from wall to wall with sand – so that he could bowl to his heart's content, whenever, and for as long as he chose. Another man (a neighbour of the impassioned Pétanque player?) smuggled a dairy calf into his home during a food shortage – so that at least his family could have milk. But the calf grew too big for the house, & too big even to get up the stairs. Nothing fazed, the man killed it, made a fine daube, and opened a restaurant, which is still there to this day. Or so they tell it in the streets of the Vieux Port.

'... tonight we can take this fish to Henri's place. It's a little bistrot on the port which has a secret recipe for Bouillabaisse. He makes a big mystery of it, but everybody knows
what it is: he perfumes the broth with cream of sea-urchin
coral ... you'll see, it's fabulous...'
From 'César' by Marcel Pagnol

*B*ouillabaisse began as poor fisherman's grub – a catch-all
of anything too little, too spiny, or too ugly to sell. It was
boiled up in water & olive oil & eaten with fingers, bread
& gusto. This maritime stew, with the characteristic Marseilles additions of garlic, fennel, tomatoes & the hot
pepper sauce called rouille, came to be known as Bouillabaisse, or in Provençal Boui-abaisso because, when the pot
boils (boui), you turn down (abaisso) the fire. In other
words, the broth must boil fast, to bind the olive oil &
water, but not for so long that the fish overcooks.

*M*arseilles is a city where every fish stall with more than
one chair claims to serve authentic Bouillabaisse, & the
recipe has been so debased that a group of Marseillais fishermen, restaurateurs & journalists finally wrote a chart to
establish the soup's essential ingredients once & for all. But of
all the cafés & restaurants in Marseilles only 13 have kept to
the relatively simple guidelines set down in this chart. Under-
standably. Any Claude, Marc or Henri can wave a watery
broth over some seaweed & call it 'la vraie Bouillabaisse', but
it takes time & care to make a real one. You won't be able to
cook it away from the Mediterranean, but it is interesting
to read this authentic Marseilles recipe.

*C*harte de la Bouillabaisse Marseillaise:
It is impossible to formalize a recipe which has
always depended on the skill of individual chefs for its
success. However, Bouillabaisse has some ingredients
which are essential if one wishes to respect the dish's
history, not just fool unsuspecting clients.

*S*ervice: In general it is served in two plates, fish in one &
broth in the other. Although these may be eaten separately,
depending on personal preference, the fish must never be cut

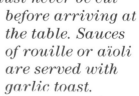

before arriving at
the table. Sauces
of rouille or aïoli
are served with
garlic toast.

Ingredients: The distinctive taste of a Marseilles Bouilla-baisse depends on the presence of a variety of Mediterra-nean fish (especially the strange local rockfish, rascasse). It is their particular aroma on which the dish's fame rests & without which it is just another fish soup.

The fish must include at least four of the following (preferably more), extremely fresh: rascasse, rascasse blanche; vive araignée (weever fish); galinette/grondin (red gurnard); St Pierre (John Dory); baudroie/lotte (anglerfish/monk-fish); fiéla/congre (conger eel); scorpène/rascasse rouge (scorpion fish).

Optional: Cigale de Mer (flat lobster); langouste (spiny rock lobster or crawfish).

Other ingredients: salt, pepper, saffron, olive oil, garlic, onions, fennel, parsley, potatoes, tomatoes.

And absolutely essential for the stock: small rockfish.

La Bouillabaisse · Marseillaise (6) ·

8–9 LB/4 KG OF THE FOLLOWING (ACCORDING TO THE MARKET):

3 LB/1.5 KG RASCASSE, 2 LB/1 KG ST PIERRE, 6 SLICES CONGRE, 3 GALINETTES, 4 VIVE ARAIGNÉES, 6 SLICES BAUDROIE

2 LB/1 KG SMALL ROCKFISH

OLIVE OIL, ONIONS, GARLIC, TOMATOES, FENNEL, PARSLEY, SALT & PEPPER, POTATOES, SAFFRON

Soften the onion, garlic and tomatoes in olive oil. Add the rockfish, cleaned & scaled, & stir for about 15 minutes until a thick paste-like consistency is reached. Moisten with boiling water & let cook at least 1 hour. Add fennel, parsley, salt & pepper and reduce to a purée. Sieve this, pressing down well to extract all the juice. Return to the heat & add the raw potatoes, cut in thick slices (2 per person), and the fish, one at a time according to their size & the firmness of their flesh: rascasse, St Pierre, congre, baudroie. Let boil 20 minutes. Five minutes before serving add the galinettes and vive araignées. When cooked, remove all the fish and the potatoes from the broth, season with salt, pepper and saffron and serve.

· *La Rouille* ·

The most usual recipe for this sauce is to add hot peppers and a pinch of saffron to aïoli (page 12), but there is another, substituting mashed potatoes for the aïoli.

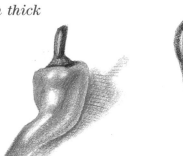

*M*arseilles' oldest fish market, on the quai de Rive Neuve, may now be a theatre (it closed for lack of space) but fishmongers travel from as far as the Italian coast to shop at the new 'Criée' of La Somati on the Route de l'Estaque. They have to get up early to beat Jean-Michel Minguella of the Miramar restaurant. He is at La Somati every morning before returning to the Vieux Port for his daily stroll along the twenty wooden fish stalls on the Quai des Belges in front of the Miramar. Here, the stalls are painted with the fishermen's boat names and the fish are more expensive, but that much fresher – straight from the net into Jean-Michel's pot. He cooks in accordance with the Charte de la Bouillabaisse, and his restaurant has long been one of the most respected by Marseillais. The freshest fish is steamed over seaweed or baked in a golden salt crust, whole sea bass is flamed over fennel, and little poached dumplings of red mullet are served with a purée of fresh sea-urchins. The brothers Minguella run the restaurant – Jean-Michel in kitchen & Pierre in the dining room. Both are mines of gastronomic knowledge.

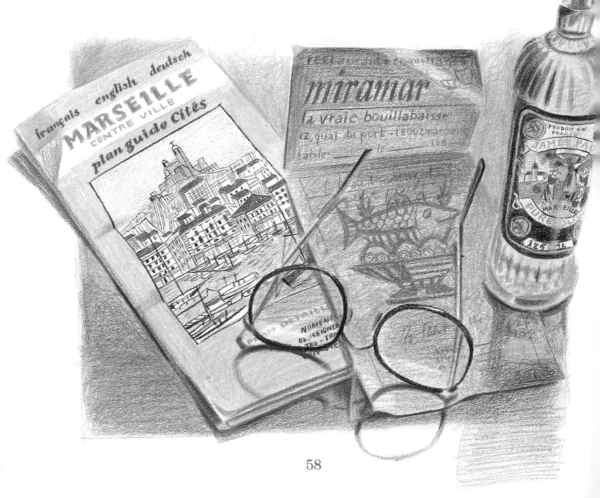

FILET de PAGRE GRILLÉ au BEURRE de PISSALA (ou POUTARGUE) et POULPES d'OLIVES NOIRES

grilled couch's sea bream or red porgy with anchovy butter & olive purée (4)

Pierre Minguella says the pagre is a 'bâlard', half-way between the pageot rouge (pandora) & the sar. A bastard the pagre may be, but as a member of the highly-prized bream family (the only Mediterranean member available on the Atlantic's western side), its firm, delicious flesh is superb when baked or, as in this recipe, grilled with salty anchovies. Daurade (gilthead bream), the pagre's more illustrious cousin, may be substituted (or any fleshy salt-water fish), with equally fine results.

4 FISH OF 14 OZ/400 G EACH OR
   2 OF 1 LB 12 OZ/800 G, CUT
   IN FILLETS

1 TSP/5 ML OF FENNEL SEEDS

OLIVE OIL

SALT & BLACK PEPPER

7 OZ/200 G BUTTER

3 TBSP/45 ML PISSALA OR
   POUTARGUE (COMMERCIAL

ANCHOVY PASTE MAY BE SUB-
   STITUTED)

7 OZ/200 G BLACK OLIVES (PREFER-
   ABLY THE SMALL ONES FROM
   NICE), STONED & CRUSHED

FRESH CHERVIL FOR DECORATION

Preheat the oven to 425°F/220°C/ gas 7. Sprinkle the fillets with fennel seeds and grill them briefly under high heat on each side. Lay them in a greased ovenproof dish, brush them with oil and season with fresh black pepper. Cook in a hot oven for 4 or 5 minutes. Meanwhile prepare the anchovy butter: pound the butter and anchovy paste together until smooth. Boil 2 fl oz/50 ml of water and add the butter, stirring all the time until melted and blended. Heat the olives in a little olive oil, just enough to make a creamy paste. To serve, lay the fillets on plates, skin down. Pour some of the anchovy butter over each and spoon a little olive paste next to them. Decorate with fresh chervil.

Petits Boudins de Rouget
· au Beurre de Cerfeuil ·
little red mullet sausages
in chervil butter (4)

Red mullet are called the wild game of the sea in Provence because they are often grilled like wild birds, with their innards intact. Here their silvery-pink skin provides the casing for a whiting mousse.

6 RED MULLET, CLEANED &
SCALED, HEADS, TAILS &
GILLS REMOVED BUT
LIVERS RESERVED

3 OZ/75 G WHITING

1 SMALL SLICE OF CRUSTLESS
BREAD SOAKED IN 5 FL OZ/
150 ML CRÈME FRAÎCHE
OR DOUBLE/HEAVY
CREAM

1 EGG, WHITE, BEATEN

SALT & PEPPER

7 OZ/200 G BUTTER

1 BUNCH FRESH CHER-
VIL, CHOPPED

· COURT BOUILLON ·

3 PT/1½ LITRES COLD
WATER

1 CARROT, SLICED

1 ONION, SLICED

2 GARLIC CLOVES

2 TBSP/30 ML
COGNAC

Fillet the red mullet into 2, keeping the skin on 8 fillets. Make a stuffing by puréeing the whiting, the mullet livers & skinless fillets. Beat in the bread & when the mixture is smooth, fold in the cream & then the beaten egg white. Season with salt & pepper. Cut 4 pieces of muslin approximately 8 in/20 cm square & on each piece lay one mullet fillet, skin side down. Divide the stuffing mixture in 4 & spoon some along each fillet. Cover with remaining 4 fillets, skin side up & roll each in the muslin to form a sausage shape. Secure the ends tightly with thread. Bring the water to the boil with the court bouillon ingredients, reduce heat to low & poach the fish for 15 mins. In the meantime, melt the butter & heat the chervil in it. When the fish has finished cooking, remove the muslin carefully, & serve the 'sausages' in a spoonful of melted chervil butter.

· PISSALA AND POUTARGUE ·

Poutargue is the roe of grey mullet that has been washed in seawater, dried, salted & pressed under a weight for 1–2 days. Rinsed & dried again, it becomes a poor man's caviare. Pissala is a strong-tasting paste made from half grown sardines & anchovies preserved in brine.

· LA BAGATELLE ·

*A*ndré Boretti, food & wine critic for Le Provençal newspaper, teacher, local historian & story-teller, is a Pagnolian figure who regards with amused scepticism foreigners' over-enthusiastic comments about Marseilles. Yet he has himself a deep, if grudging, love for his home town & its inhabitants. And the feeling is mutual; the coquillage vendor in the market offers a fresh sea-urchin to him in passing, he is hailed in the streets with grins & waves from restaurant & café-owners of every nationality. André is highly critical of most Marseilles restaurants: 'These days they charge too much for too little. And most of them mangent la grenouille (Marseilles slang for doing something badly) anyway!' But for one young chef, Pierre Bagatelle of the diminutive 'La Bagatelle' restaurant, he has nothing but unreserved admiration.

· BLANCMANGER de · CASTELGRAMBOIS
almond & monkfish mousse (4)

Pierre Bagatelle's cooking ranges from classic Provençal brandade de morue to a brilliantly inventive chilled artichoke soufflé with smoked cod sauce. For one special dinner André Boretti helped him create a menu using only fourteenth & fifteenth-century recipes – including this one from the fourteenth-century chef Taillevent's rare book 'Le Viandier'.

FOR SALT-WATER FISH *

2 LB/1 KG LOTTE/MONKFISH OR 2 GOOD-SIZED BREAM OR SIMILAR FLESHY SALT-WATER FISH, CLEANED, SKINNED AND/OR SCALED
A LITTLE BUTTER
1 WINEGLASS SHERRY, NOILLY BLANC OR DRY WHITE WINE
3–4 SMALL ONIONS, PEELED
½ BAY LEAF
BRANCH OF DILL <u>OR</u>

1 TSP FENNEL SEEDS
JUICE OF 1 LIME
½ TSP/2.5 ML GROUND GINGER
1 TSP/5 ML SUGAR
4 OZ/125 G GROUND ALMONDS
1–2 TBSP CRÈME FRAÎCHE OR DOUBLE/HEAVY CREAM
SEVERAL TOASTED ALMONDS TO DECORATE

* Fresh-water fish may be used instead but the dill/fennel seeds above should be replaced with a few sprigs of thyme or a very few grains of cardamom, crushed.

Step 1: Preheat oven to 180°C/ 350°F/gas 4. Rinse the fish rapidly under cold water & dry very well with a cotton towel. Butter an ovenproof dish & lay the fish in it. Dot fish with butter. Add the sherry, onions, bay leaf and dill. Cook the fish in the oven until just tender, about 25–30 mins. When cooked,

(continued on next page)

· LOUP à la VAPEUR ·
d'ALGUES MARINES

*sea bass steamed
whole on
seaweed (2–4)*

*If there is one thing
the Marseillais do
very well, it is to
cook fish simply and
beautifully – maxi-
mizing the essential
fishiness and mini-
mizing what André
Boretti calls the
'tra-la-la'. The best
known Provençal fish
recipe is sea bass
grilled over fennel
branches, flamed at
the last minute.
This recipe, in
which the fish
virtually swims
through a steam
bath of seaweed onto
your plate, is just as good –
provided that you start with
very fresh fish. Pierre Bagatelle
cooks turbot in a similar way,
but steams it over lime blossoms instead. Almost any mild
herb works well, but nothing
preserves the fish's taste so well
as seaweed.*

1 SEA BASS OF ABOUT 14 OZ – 1 LB/ 350–450 G CLEANED & SCALED BUT WITH HEAD & TAIL STILL ON
COARSE SEA SALT & BLACK PEPPER
1 GENEROUS GLASS DRY WHITE WINE (EG FROM CASSIS)
OLIVE OIL

remove bones and reserve the
cooking juices.

Step 2: Blend together well the
lime juice, ginger, sugar and
almonds with the cooking juices
and the fish and onion. The
mixture should be quite thick.
Add the cream and stir well.
Pour the mixture into a lightly
buttered terrine and cover with
foil. Cook in a bain-marie for
10–15 minutes in the oven. To
serve, run a knife around the
edge of the terrine and tip out
onto a plate. Decorate with
toasted almonds.

2 TBSP/30 ML CRÈME FRAÎCHE OR
  DOUBLE/HEAVY CREAM

ENOUGH WELL-RINSED SEAWEED TO
  MAKE A THICK BED FOR THE FISH
  & A FISH KETTLE WITH STEAMER
  BIG ENOUGH TO HOLD THE FISH*

*If you do not have a steamer,
a fish kettle packed with a thick
layer of seaweed works fairly
well, in which case not much
water is needed. Alternatively
you could use a wok with a
layer of fennel branches at the
bottom to keep the seaweed and
fish clear of the water.

Score the fish with 3 diagonal
slashes and rub it inside and
out with sea salt. Pack the
steamer with seaweed, lay the
fish on top and place it in the
kettle with the wine and about
½ in/1.5 cm of boiling water.
Drizzle olive oil over the fish,
cover tightly and steam for
15–20 minutes, depending on
the thickness of the fish. To
serve, lift the fish onto a hot
serving plate and pile the seaweed around it. Turn the heat
up under the cooking liquid
and when it is reduced to
about a coffee-cupful, stir in
the cream and season with salt
& pepper. Pour a little over the
fish and serve the rest in a
separate jug.

How to tell if your fish is fresh:
The eye should be brilliant and
rounded, not sunken. Gently
touch the side of the fish with
your fingertips – if skin is slip-
pery, even a little sticky, it was
caught within the last 24 hrs.

DAURADE au GROS SEL
sea bream baked in a
salt crust (4)

The golden fish-shaped salt
crust in this recipe is not
merely decorative. The salt acts
like clay to seal in the fish
juices and aroma and cut
down the cooking time.

1 2 LB/1 KG SEA BREAM, CLEANED
  & SCALED BUT HEAD & TAIL
  LEFT ON

FOR SALT CRUST

SEA SALT

FLOUR

WARM WATER

Preheat the oven to 450°F/
230°C/gas 8. Make the salt paste
by adding 3 tbsp/45 ml four
and 3–4 tbsp/45–60 ml warm
water to every 8 oz/250 g salt
used. You will need about 2 lb/
1 kg salt to cover a 2 lb/1 kg
fish. Lay the fish on an oval
fireproof serving dish and
cover it with a layer of paste
about ½ in/12 mm thick. With
the edge of a spoon draw the
eyes, tail, gills and scales on
the paste and bake for 20 minutes. Serve straight from the
dish. The crust, which becomes
hard and golden brown in the
oven, should be cracked open at
the very last minute.

· A CORSICAN CONNECTION ·

*O*ver the past century or so since Napoleon quit his birth-place to relocate in grander premises to the north, Marseilles has become virtually the second capital of Corsica. Madame Rolande Ségala has lived in Marseilles for a long time but still cooks this melting Corsican cheesecake, as her mother & grandmother did before her. The cake is the richer bourgeois version of Fiadonetti – tiny pastry tarts made by the Corsican peasants and spread with a similar cheese filling. (Ricotta may be substituted for Brousse, but the cake will not taste so richly of cheese.)

· FIADONE ·
(GÂTEAU à la BROUSSE)
Corsican cheesecake with caramel

Brousse, or the Corsican equivalent Broccio, was made by boiling goat or ewe's milk & adding strong white vinegar, causing the milk to curdle instantly. The Brousse vendors used to come from the small town of Rove, with big wicker platters of the fresh cheeses slung around their necks. Their cry of 'Brousse, Brousse de Rove', & the toot of their trumpets, was known up & down the streets of Marseilles. Certain gourmets on the old port considered the cheese such a delicacy that they used to reserve one Brousse each before beginning dinner, for fear that there would be none left by dessert. A few Brousse vendors still sell the real ewe's milk cheese in Marseilles' markets, but except in Corsica it is now usually made of cow's milk & sold in plastic colanders.

· CARAMEL SAUCE ·

3 OZ/75 G CASTER SUGAR
4 FL OZ/100 ML WATER
4 OZ/100 G CASTER SUGAR
3 FL OZ/75 ML MILK
12 OZ/350 G BROUSSE CHEESE (RICOTTA OR SIMILAR DRY SOFT CURD CHEESE WILL DO) CRUSHED WITH A FORK
ZEST OF 1 LEMON, GRATED
6 EGGS

Preheat the oven to 325°F/100°C/ gas 3. Caramellize a 7 in × 3 in/ 180 mm × 75 mm (approximate) cake tin by heating the sugar and water together over medium heat. Once the syrup has reached boiling point do not stir but continue to let it boil gently until it turns golden brown, then swirl the caramel round so it coats the sides of the tin. To make the cake, heat the remaining sugar in the milk until just under boiling. Let cool. Stir little by little into the cheese, blending well. Add the lemon zest, then beat in the eggs, one by one. Pour this into the caramellized cake tin & stand it in a pan of hot water. (The water should come half-way up the cake tin.) Bake for 1 hour (or until set) in the oven. Tip the cake upside down onto a dish. If the caramel sauce does not come out with it, heat another tablespoon of water in the tin until the remaining caramel dissolves. Pour this over the cake and serve with chilled Beaumes-de-Venise or Corsican muscat.

• Limaçons •

Limaçons are thumbnail-size snails gathered on the wild fennel by roadsides. They are laborious to prepare, like all snails, being first fed on fennel & flour for 10–12 days to clean them, then washed in running water until they stop frothing, & finally boiled in a broth of fennel, orange & garlic for 3–4 hours. If this seems like a hard fortnight's work for the end result, look for Giselle, in the Avenue du Prado market, the last of a long line of limaçon-sellers in Marseilles. She will sell you a ladleful of her cooked speciality straight from the pot, just as her predecessors did all over Provence.

• MOUSSE aux POIREAUX •

In Provence fish is often served with aïoli or with a hot sauce such as rouille. Both are good with salt cod or strong-tasting fish soup, but can overpower delicate red mullet and bream. At Faucigny, one of the oldest & best of Marseilles' restaurants a row of grilled red mullets appears with a bowl of crème fraîche into which is beaten salt, pepper & puréed cooked leeks.

•Chez Étienne•

If you climb the eery covered stairway that leads up from the rue de la République into Marseilles' old town, you will find a doorway marked Pizzaria immediately on your left. Inside, Étienne presides over what is a Marseilles institution, not just for pizza, but for aubergines in tomatoes, cheese & garlic, tiny cuttlefish fried simply but well in oil & parsley, & (best of all) tender lamb skewered on whole branches of rosemary, a method of adding herbs from the inside out that gives the meat a subtle aroma without overpowering it.

*E*ven if you hate mar-
zipan with a passion,
if your liver twinges at
the mention of almond
paste and your heart
burns, still you will
have to eat calissons
in Aix-en-Provence.
As early as the 1500s the
Provençal poet Claude Bruyes
was extolling the virtues
of Aix's calissons,
and by the end of
the 1600s they were
being distributed to
the faithful every year on
September 1st, to commemorate
the end of the great plague of
1630. The whole Cours Mirabeau
is devoted to this famous
almond and melon paste sweetmeat. There are at least four
confiseries that specialize in
them. Even the bookshops on
the Cours sell books cleverly
designed to introduce a 'History
of the Calissons of Aix' into
their plots. Nowhere can you be
lured more easily into the pur-
chase of your first calissons
than at the lovely chocolate-
box of a shop 'A la Reine
Jeanne' at 36 Cours Mirabeau.
The mingled smells of newly-
ground almonds and sugared
fruits, and the charm of
Monique and her sister (and
brother Joseph in the kitchens),
fifth generation of the same
family to make calissons, are
irresistible.

60mm

25mm

CALISSONS d'AIX
almond & melon paste sweet cakes

Provence produces the
sweetest almonds
in Europe and
Aix is the un-
challenged
almond capital of
Provence. Its calissons have
been awarded an
Appellation Con-
trôlée (like fine
wine) for their quality. Popu-
larized commercially between
1830–1860, when the confec-
tioners and pastry-makers of
Aix first began to be known all
over France, they are made
with a proportion of 40%
blanched almonds, pounded
and slow-baked with 60% glacé
melons and fruit syrup. For
this blending process special
machines are used. The following recipe, adapted from the
1896 cookbook by J B Reboul,
'La Cuisinière Provençale',
produces a not unsatisfactory
home version.

131 mm

9 OZ/250 G FINE GRANULATED
  SUGAR

11 OZ/300 G POWDERED ALMONDS

2 TBSP/30 ML GLACÉ MELON,
  CRUSHED

2–3 TBSP/30–45 ML APRICOT OR
  OTHER SYRUP

RICE PAPER

• GLACE ROYALE •
(ROYAL ICING)

7 OZ/200 G ICING SUGAR

2 EGG WHITES

Pound the sugar and almonds together finely in a mortar. Sieve & return to mortar. Work in glacé melon & enough fruit syrup to make a smooth paste. Flatten slightly, place in a dish & in a very low oven dry paste to the consistency of stiff pastry dough. Spread $\frac{1}{4}$ in/6 mm thick over rice paper. Make royal icing by beating icing sugar & egg-whites with a wooden spoon until a smooth, shiny paste is formed. Spread this over calisson mixture in a very thin layer & when set, cut calissons into elongated ovals of about $1\frac{1}{2}$ in/35 mm (see drawing). Dry out again for 10–15 mins in a moderate oven.

Add ground aniseed if used. Add liquid egg whites & work into the dry mixture

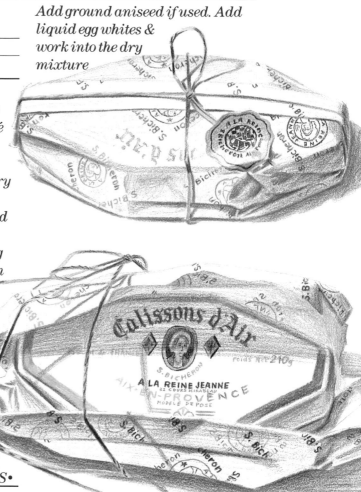

•CROISSANTS aux PIGNONS•
sweet crescents rolled in pine nuts

These firm, moist almond biscuits mentioned by the prophet Nostradamus in 1552 are familiar all over Provence, but nowhere are they better than in Aix.

9 OZ/250 G GRANULATED SUGAR

9 OZ/250 G POWDERED ALMONDS

1 TSP/5 ML GROUND ANISEED (OR CUMIN), OPTIONAL

3 EGG WHITES

2–3 OZ/50–75 G PINE KERNELS/ NUTS, TOASTED

Preheat oven to 325°F/170°C/gas 3. Pound together in a mortar, then sieve, sugar & powdered almonds.

until you obtain a firm, smooth dough. Form into crescent-moon shapes about $1\frac{1}{2}$ in/35 mm long & $\frac{3}{4}$ in/20 mm thick. Roll these in the toasted pine nuts & bake on a buttered floured tray for one hour – or until the croissants are dry. Stored in a well-sealed container, they will keep for several months.

· CLOS DE LA VIOLETTE ·

*A*ix-en-Provence is a good town for pâtisseries – some of the best in France – but surprisingly, considering Aix's patrician history as a political and artistic centre, not for regional restaurants. One of only a few exceptions is the Clos de la Violette, a rambling old house in quiet back-streets near Cézanne's old studio. The owner and chef, Jean-Marc Banzo, left his home town of Vaison-la-Romaine at the age of 15 to work as a cook all over Provence. Inspired by recipes found in old cookbooks, he developed his own style, appropriately as elegant as Aix itself. Jean-Marc has the traditional Provençal respect for vegetables, which he shops for in Aix's delightful market square, the Place Richelme, and has just planted his own herb and vegetable garden. 'Right now it gives more work than vegetables,' Jean-Marc said ruefully, 'but this summer – the best basil in Provence!'

BARIGOULE d'ARTICHAUTS en TERRINE au COULIS de · POIVRONS ROUGES ·

terrine of artichokes & young vegetables in a red pepper purée (8)

'Barigoule' or 'berigoulo' is the old Provençal generic term for agaric mushrooms. Artichokes cooked à la barigoule once meant that they were trimmed, moistened with generous ladles of olive oil and grilled whole over a fire –

8 OZ/250 G GOOD MUSHROOMS, SLICED

3 YOUNG CARROTS, CUT IN STRIPS
   LENGTHWISE

8 OZ/250 G BABY ONIONS OR
   SHALLOTS, PEELED

2 RIPE TOMATOES, PEELED, SEEDED
   & CHOPPED

1 PT/500 ML WHITE WINE

SPRIG OF THYME & 1 BAY LEAF, TIED
   TOGETHER

SALT & PEPPER

5 SHEETS OF GELATINE,
   SOFTENED IN A LITTLE
   COLD WATER
   (POWERDERED GELA-
   TINE IS NOT SO
   SUCCESSFUL)

½ PT/250 ML OLIVE
   OIL

• COULIS – PEPPER PURÉE •

5 BIG RED PEPPERS

BASIL

SALT & PEPPER

OLIVE OIL

'Aix. A blind man thinks it rains;
Could he see without his cane
He'd see a hundred blue fountains
Singing the praises of Cézanne.'
          Jean Cocteau, 1919

the way mushrooms of the same name would have been cooked. The term à la barigoule is now a catch-all for any recipe in which artichokes are cooked with thyme, mushrooms or ham. Jean-Marc Banzo begins with the old recipe and turns it into this beautiful layered vegetable terrine.

4 OZ/100 G SMOKED BACON,
   CHOPPED

5 GARLIC CLOVES, CRUSHED

2 LEEKS, TRIMMED & CHOPPED

24 ARTICHOKE HEARTS (SMALL
   PROVENÇAL VIOLET ONES FOR
   PREFERENCE OR 8–10 LARGER
   ONES) *

* You can use tinned artichoke hearts (in which case they do not need to be cooked with the other vegetables), but the dish will not be so good.

In a heavy-based pan big enough to hold all the ingredients, cook the bacon until the fat has just begun to run. Add the garlic & the leeks, cook until softened, and then all the vegetables (except the peppers). Turn them gently in the pan for several minutes. Add the wine, thyme and bay, cover and cook over medium heat for 30–45 mins. In the meantime gently heat the olive oil and mix with

(continued on next page)

the softened gelatine. When the vegetables are just tender, remove from heat, allow to cool slightly, drain off their liquid & add this to the gelatine mixture.

METHOD 1: To make a decorative layered terrine, spoon one layer of gelatine into a deep terrine & chill for 10 mins. Place the artichoke hearts in rows on top (if using larger ones cut in quarters) and cover with a thin layer of gelatine. Chill again, then arrange the carrots lengthwise on top. Chill for another 10 minutes, arrange the onions in rows, cover with mushrooms, rest of vegetable mixture in pan and the remaining gelatine. Chill for 24 hours.

METHOD 2: for a simpler vegetable terrine, mix the gelatine (dissolved in oil) into the vegetables thoroughly, then pour into a terrine and chill for 24 hours.

Before serving, grill the red peppers, remove peel and seeds and purée. Season with chopped basil, salt and pepper and enough olive oil to make the mixture liquid. Remove the terrine from its dish by dipping the base into hot water. Spoon a little sauce on to each plate and on top lay a thin slice of terrine. Serve chilled.

CRÉPINETTES d'AGNEAU des ALPILLES à la CRÈME d'AIL
noisettes of lamb with ratatouille & creamy garlic sauce (4)

Two places particularly noted for their excellent lamb are Sisteron, a mountain town in the high rough country near Provence's north-east border, & the range of low hills called Les Alpilles, south-west of St Rémy. In this dish the tender lamb of the Alpilles is enclosed in a cushion of the Provençal vegetable stew ratatouille and cooked quickly to seal in precious juices.

1 BONED SADDLE OF LAMB, CUT INTO 4 NOISETTES OF 5 OZ/150 G EACH

11 OZ/300 G CAUL FAT, SOAKED IN TEPID WATER TO SOFTEN

SALT & PEPPER

11 OZ/300 G RATATOUILLE, MADE 12 HOURS BEFORE (SEE RECIPE)

OLIVE OIL

11 OZ/300 G GARLIC CLOVES, PEELED & COOKED GENTLY UNTIL SOFT IN

4 FL OZ/100 ML CRÈME FRAÎCHE (OR DOUBLE/HEAVY CREAM)

2–3 TBSP/30–45 ML MEAT STOCK

Preheat the oven to 400°F/ 200°C/gas 6. Season both sides of the noisettes with salt and pepper. Cut caul fat into 4, spoon a little mashed ratatouille onto each piece & lay the lamb on top. Spoon over the remaining ratatouille and lap the edges of the caul fat over well. Over a high heat, brown both sides of the parcels in a little oil in a flameproof casserole. Finish off for 10 mins in the oven. Drain off excess fat and keep the lamb warm. Mash the softened garlic cloves and sieve the garlic cream sauce into the lamb casserole. Stir in several spoonfuls of stock (enough to make the mixture liquid), simmer for a couple of minutes and season with salt and pepper. Pour a little sauce over each noisette and serve very hot.

· *RATATOUILLE* ·
Provençal vegetable stew

Ratatouille is perhaps the most famous Provençal vegetable dish, and also the one most often made badly. The purplish-grey mess incorrectly called ratatouille in many restaurants bears no resemblance to the real brightly gleaming stew. Here each vegetable is cooked separately to conserve its aroma & then they are just simmered together gently at the end. This takes a bit longer than the old bung everything-in-the-pot method but can be made in generous quantities to serve cold the next day.

1 LB/500 G AUBERGINES, CUT IN ½ IN/12 MM SLICES
SALT & PEPPER
OLIVE OIL
1 LB/500 G COURGETTES, CUT IN SMALL CHUNKS
1 LB/500 G MIXED RED & GREEN PEPPERS, CORED & SLICED THINLY
8 OZ/250 G ONIONS, PEELED & FINELY CHOPPED
1½ LB/750 G TOMATOES, PEELED, SEEDED & CHOPPED
3 CLOVES GARLIC, PEELED & FINELY CHOPPED
½ TSP/2.5 ML SUGAR
HANDFUL OF PARSLEY, FINELY CHOPPED
LEAVES FROM SEVERAL SPRIGS OF THYME
9–10 BASIL LEAVES, CUT IN STRIPS

Salt the aubergines and leave for 30 minutes to drain. Pat dry and cut into small chunks. Heat about 6 tbsp/90 ml of olive oil in a large heavy-based frying pan. Add the aubergines and when brown on all sides, remove and drain on paper towels. Add a little more oil and cook the courgettes in the pan until all their moisture has evaporated. Remove and drain.

Continue with the peppers, removing them when tender. Add the onions, cook until soft but not brown. Stir in the tomatoes, garlic, sugar, parsley & thyme & simmer for about 30 mins. Add the rest of the vegetables and after 5 mins remove from heat, mix in the basil & refrigerate overnight.

Four excellent wines to enjoy from this region are the elegant Palette from CHÂTEAU SIMONE; CHÂTEAU VIGNELAURE & DOMAINE TEMPIER'S rich & heady reds; and the delightful DOMAINE LES BASTIDES.

A TASTE OF THE SEA IN MARSEILLES

MARSEILLES' QUAI DE RIVE NEUVE IS LINED WITH 'DÉGUSTATION COQUILLAGES' SIGNS. THE LUSCIOUS, SALTY OYSTERS 'CÔTES BLEUES' ARE PREFERRED, OR SPIKY SEA-URCHINS CUT OPEN TO REVEAL OZONE-SWEET MOUTHFULS OF CORAL. ONLY REAL SHELLFISH FANS CAN FACE THE FUNGUS-LIKE EXTERIOR OF THE VIOLET OR FIGUE DE MER (SEA FIG). CUT OPEN IT REVEALS A SPONGY GREY INTERIOR FILLED WITH WHAT COULD ONLY POLITELY BE DESCRIBED AS VERY WET SCRAMBLED EGGS. THIS, SCOOPED OUT WITH THE THUMB & CONSUMED, STILL QUIVERING, WITHOUT BENEFIT OF BREAD OR LEMON, REWARDS THE COURAGEOUS WITH AN OVERPOWERING BUT DELICIOUS TASTE OF THE SEA – EVEN BETTER THAN OYSTERS.

Black bulls on a
WIDE PLAIN

*S*t-Rémy-
de-Provence
is everyone's idea of the quintessential Provençal
town: a café or two on every corner and a pot of geraniums
in every window. On market day Citroën vans carrying
precariously-balanced baskets of produce squeeze past
one another in their rush to get to a market square
strung with red, white & blue flags. The town should
be haunted, but isn't, by the Romans, who built their own
town of Glanum, and a cenotaph to their Emperor Augustus' grandsons, just to the south; or at least by Van Gogh –
he spent the last year of his life in St-Rémy's mental
asylum.

*F*rom St-Rémy through Arles to the Camargue plain
is Van Gogh country – broad yellow fields spattered
with blood-red poppies, ditches of wild irises, dead-
straight roads & small towns of red-tiled blue-shuttered
houses. North of Arles, a series of low limestone hills, the
Alpilles, rises abruptly. They are mysterious in any light:
eery, shimmering silver under the moon, bleached-dry
white in the glare of the Provençal sun. Approached from
the St-Rémy road the Alpilles' castle of Les Baux looms,
its windows empty as a skull's eye-sockets. Here in the
fourteenth century lived Raymond de Turenne, who was
known to weep with joy while throwing his adversaries
from the walls; and the unspeakable Bérengère, who forced

his wife to eat the heart & blood of her secret lover. Madame Bérengère, in the romantic tradition of the Provençal Troubadour, declared that never again would she eat so sweet a dish, & promptly threw herself over the castle walls. None of these ghosts from past tragedies appears to haunt the famous restaurant L'Oustau de Baumanière, at the base of Les Baux, unless they are the ghosts of tourists who died wandering through the castle's present maze of souvenir shops.

*F*rom Les Baux to Arles, the road winds south through vineyards, olive trees & sleepy villages. Go mid-week to avoid the bullfights & sit in Arles' arena that has stood since the Romans built it 2000 years ago. The sun should be hot enough to give you a slight headache, & the glare of it off the hard white ground makes dark glasses not fashion but necessity. Go when only the flies & not the crowds are buzzing, & even then you won't be alone. In the arena below there will certainly be at least two boys, almost men, but still as thin & scrappy as whippets. They have come to practise their fighting passes – one to be bullfighter & the other bull – throughout the afternoon. At first it seems slightly comic; an arrogant youngster with a heavy scarlet cape, his head bent at the classic toreador's angle to watch his friend, whose two fingers are above his head as horns. But the heat builds; the flies' buzzing, the shouts of 'Eh-taureau!' from the slim bullfighter, the grunts & slow wheeling turns of the 'bull' create a rhythm that is as tense as any real Sunday afternoon corrida with its taped music and busloads of tourists.

*G*o to Arles in the early morning of a Wednesday or Saturday for the most famous market in Provence; buy walnut & honey tarts laid out in flat wicker baskets; 'lou cachat', that gamy buried cheese that is better for clearing the sinuses than smelling salts; famous spicy saucisson d'Arles from a huge selection in a mobile chrome butcher's shop, cold-pressed olive oil & pinkish-grey Listel wine from the Camargue's salt marshes. If you are lucky, the man who sells his own terracotta pottery will be there, & you can fill a traditional rust-brown gratin dish with plump aubergines & peppers. But when the sun gets too high, when the fate of those dear fluffy rabbits at the next stall gets too close for comfort & a hundred people in the crowded market seem to know your body better than you do yourself, leave the Boulevard des Lices (which means Lists as in jousting, <u>not</u> lice) for the church of Saint-Trophime. Off the little sun-baked Place de la République you enter the Middle Ages – the eternally beautiful cloisters of St Trophimus, carved by master sculptors from the 12th to the 14th centuries, silent enough for you to hear dust fall.

*A*rles is the beginning of the Camargue, a wide, flat delta, half marshy wilderness, half rich agricultural ranchland, that is embraced by two arms of the Rhône as it flows to meet the Mediterranean. Here black, long-horned fighting bulls, so fierce that no wily Camarguais horse will meet them in the ring (Spanish horses are imported for the corridas), are tended by Provençal cow-boys – 'gardians'. Pink flamingoes stand one-legged in summer rice-paddies that shimmer like mirages as far as the low horizon, & in autumn, newly-harvested fennel makes the air smell of pastis. It is a landscape from the banks of the Nile or the Tigris. And the people of the Camargue could well have come from those eastern deltas: olive-skinned with date-brown eyes, their food is a mixture of gipsy inventiveness & maritime plenty. After the bullfights in Arles nothing is wasted. The bulls are butchered, sold as viande de taureau in the markets, & simmered long & slowly with orange or ancho-vies. In July, when Méjanes holds its annual fiesta, bulls are roasted whole over huge barbecues – tended by specialists who know how to tenderize the toughest meat. On the coast, at Saintes-Maries-de-la Mer, where the gipsies come twice a year to commemorate their black Saint Sarah, and at the excellent La Camargue restaurant in the strangely sad little fortified town of Aigues-Mortes, there are salty-fleshed wild ducks; small clams called tellines; mussels and cuttlefish cooked with Camargue rice and fennel; and a saffroned stew of eels calls Catigot, served with flame-hot rouille sauce.

Just south of Les Baux are two of the best oil mills in Provence, one at Fontvieille, and the other, more famous – Maître Cornille's – in Maussane. It seems hardy credible that chefs from all over south-west Provence come to buy their olive oil in this quiet village that is little more than a cluster of old houses around a dusty square full of Provençal grandmothers. Until you taste the oil. And where there is good oil, there are usually good restaurants; on the main street of Maussane is 'Ou Ravi Provençau', where Jean-François Richard and his wife Aurore entertain friends, customers and extended family. Maître Cornille comes often – for Jambon Maison smoked over rosemary branches and served with home-pickled cherries, for Provençal rabbit simmered in fresh thyme, and exquisite wild strawberry ice cream. So does Flo, an ex-chef who, 20 years ago, rode to Paris on his white Camarguais horse. Both Flo and the horse saw the Tour Eiffel and drank champagne in the Café Royal. They preferred Maussane.

· BOHÉMIENNE ·
grilled aubergines/eggplants and red peppers (4)

Bohémienne is another word for gitane or gipsy, and if gipsies can ever be said to have homes, this land, especially from Arles to the sea, is theirs. No one, least of all the gipsies, seems to know why this simple dish is named as it is, although everyone willingly offers unlikely theories. It is usually prepared like a ratatouille without courgettes (zucchini), but Jean-François lifts his own version out of the ordinary by grilling instead of stewing the vegetables, & then adding a spoonful of fragrant pistou.

4 SMALL OVAL AUBERGINES/ EGGPLANTS

2 BIG RED PEPPERS

OLIVE OIL

BLACK PEPPER

1 LARGE JUICY TOMATO, PEELED & SEEDED

PISTOU SAUCE (SEE PAGE 81) MADE WITH 2 EXTRA TBSP/30 ML FRESH BASIL FOR DECORATION

Grill the aubergines and peppers until the skin is blackened & the flesh is tender right through. Cut the peppers in half, peel & seed them. Peel the aubergines but keep their stems, if they have them. Arrange the vegetables on 4 plates, pour over a little olive oil, season with coarsely ground black pepper and serve with pistou and fresh basil leaves (see drawing).

• *PERDRAU à la GITANE* •
gipsy style partridge

The gipsies of the Camargue, having stolen some fine plump chickens, would bury them whole, feathers & all in the clay under their campfires. If any suspicious farmer turned up, searching for his missing fowl, there was nothing to be seen. A few hours later, when the coast had cleared, the birds were dug up & the feathers pulled off together with the now hard-baked clay. Flo cooks quail, small chickens & partridges in a similar way: first they are cleaned & plucked, then stuffed with muscat grapes, wrapped in oiled leaves & buried in the sand under a charcoal fire for 2–3 hours. It seems worth a try. Ideally, the packed earth or sand keeps the birds moist & allows the grapes' perfume to penetrate their flesh.

77

1½ LB/550 G BOILED COD, FLAKED

SALT & BLACK PEPPER

ABOUT 24 SLIM GREEN BEANS, BOILED

3 TBSP/45 ML FRESH PARSLEY, FINELY CHOPPED

• SAUCE •

5 LARGE RIPE TOMATOES

4 TBSP/60 ML OLIVE OIL

4–8 BASIL LEAVES, CUT IN FINE STRIPS

1 TBSP/15 ML WHITE WINE VINEGAR

SALT & PEPPER

•PAIN MARTEGAU•
cod & vegetable
pâté Martigues style (6)

South-western Provence is the real heart of aïoli country. Every summer fête here has a Grand Aïoli, with huge mortars full of the shining yellow sauce and platters of salt cod & crisply-cooked vegetables. This recipe from Flo's home-town of Martigues was sup-posedly invented to use up the leftovers from one of these grandes bouffes. Really it is only an excuse for continuing the garlic party into the next day. (Although this dish would normally be made with salt cod, you can equally well use fresh.)

1¼ LB/550 G BOILED POTATOES, PEELED & SIEVED

JUICE OF 1 LEMON

4–5 TBSP/ 60–75 ML AÏOLI (PAGE 12)

First make the pâté: beat the potatoes, lemon juice & aïoli together until smooth. Stir in the cod & season with salt & lots of coarsely ground black pepper. Divide the mixture into three & press the first third into a greased 3 pint terrine or loaf tin. Lay half the beans in lengthwise strips on top. Beat parsley into the next ⅓ of aïoli mixture & press that into the tin as well. Lay the rest of the beans on top & spoon over the remaining aïoli mixture. Weigh down with a board or other suitable object that fits the inside of the tin & chill overnight. To make the sauce, peel & seed the tomatoes & purée with the other (continued on following page) ingredients. Leave in a cool place but do not chill. The next day remove the pâté from its tin by briefly dipping it in hot water. Pour a little sauce on each plate & place a thin slice of pâté on top. Serve cool.

* This recipe presumes that you will only have beans, potatoes, cod & aïoli left over; you can of course add more layered vegetables (remembering that it is only the potatoes & aïoli that give the pâté its shape), but too many different varieties tend to destroy the decorative shape.

· SOUPE au PISTOU ·
vegetable soup with garlic, basil & tomato sauce (6–8)

If you stop at Maussane on a hot summer day, & see a gaggle of old ladies shelling fresh beans in the main square, they are sure to be Jean-François' relations. 'The only way I can offer Soupe au pistou in my restaurant is if my wife's aunt & grandmother prepare the beans,' said Monsieur Richard. 'It's one of those 'simple' family dishes that takes a lot of time & must be very very fresh.' In Nice this soup is served with the basil & parmesan sauce on page 27. Here in the Arles region & in north-western Provence, pistou is made with basil & raw tomatoes to give a fresher, less rich soup. The sauce should never be cooked, just stirred in at the last minute.

---

1 LB/500 G GREEN BEANS, CUT IN
  2 IN/5 CM LENGTHS

1 LB/500 G FRESH PINTO BEANS
  OR 1 LB/500 G BROAD BEANS,
  SHELLED

1 LB/500 G FRESH WHITE
  HARICOT BEANS,
  SHELLED OR

8 OZ/250 G DRIED
  HARICOT OR
  CANNELLINI BEANS,
  SOAKED OVERNIGHT

2 POTATOES,
  PEELED AND
  ROUGHLY CHOPPED

2 TOMATOES,
  PEELED

1 LB/500 G COUR
  GETTES/ZUCCHINI,
  UNPEELED & DICED

WHITES OF TWO LEEKS, CHOPPED

LEAVES OF TWO CELERY STICKS,
  CHOPPED

SALT & PEPPER

4 OZ/100 G LARGE SHORT
MACARONI

PISTOU SAUCE

3–4 GARLIC CLOVES, PEELED

2 BIG BUNCHES FRESH BASIL *

4 OZ/100 G GRATED GRUYÈRE OR
PARMESAN

1 TOMATO, GRILLED, WITH SKIN
& PIPS REMOVED

2–3 TBSP/30–45 ML OLIVE OIL

Bring 3½ pt/2 litres of cold
water to the boil, add all vegetables except for the green
beans & courgettes. Cover and
simmer gently for 2 hours. Add
the remaining vegetables &
macaroni, more salt and
pepper if necessary, and cook
for a further 15 minutes. Alternatively, you can pre-cook the
dried beans, simmer the fresh
vegetables until tender & add
the cooked beans to the soup at
the same time as the macaroni.
In the meantime make the pistou sauce; pound the garlic &
basil together into a paste,
work in the cheese & the
grilled tomato. Add the olive
oil, a little at a time, beating
in well, & then a few spoonfuls
of the soup broth. Serve the
soup with the pistou sauce in
its mortar.

* It is a mistake to attempt
pistou with less basil – make a
different but still delicious
soup with fresh marjoram or
oregano.

· TELLINES ·
wedge shell clams

A telline is a tiny clam about
the size of a hammered thumb-
nail, the eating of which
demands perseverance. Their
fishermen, who carry wide, flat
sieves to keep the tellines in
and let the sand out, fish only
one short stretch of sand;
further out the clams lose their
salty aroma. Badly prepared,
tellines can be gritty & saltily
slimy – they need long washing
in fresh water to rid them of
sand. At their best, opened
over a high flame, allowed to
cool slightly (so that they don't
absorb oil but are only coated
in it) & tossed in parsley and
vinaigrette, they have a
refreshing taste of the ocean
that goes well with a glass of
Ricard. They are served like
this as an appetizer at the
charming Bistrot Le Paradou
near Maussane, whose tables
are crowded every Friday with
throngs of locals eating aïoli.
The regulars – mayor, electri-
cians, plumbers, wine-makers
and local aristocracy – eat
together at a long trestle table
wedged between bar and
kitchen.

So many tellines used to be bought in Arles that the peoples of that town became known as *telliniers*. And the little bivalves are still as popular at the Arles restaurant Le Vaccarès, where chef & patron Bernard Dumas serves them dry-fried with lots of garlic, whenever they are available (this isn't often, & as they never appear on the menu, it's best to ask). He is a chef's chef, what his colleagues call 'sérieux' – very genuine about his work. He feels traditional dishes are worth serving, admittedly with his own touch, 'Because they are an expression of popular culture – & besides that, they taste good! Sometimes the distinction between subtlety and blandness in modern cooking is too subtle even for the experts.'

Le Vaccarès overlooks the Place du Forum, where Van Gogh painted his 'Starry, starry night' café (now a funiture store – what price fame?). From the restaurant balcony the remnants of the Forum's Roman columns, embedded in the walls of the Hotel Nord-Pinus, are only clam-hurling distance away; but the clams at Le Vaccarès are too salty & delicious to waste.

· LOUP à la VAPEUR · à la COMPOTE d'ORANGES et de CITRONS

steamed sea bass with stewed oranges & lemons (4)

Monsieur Dumas gets his sea bass from a fisherman friend at Saintes-Maries-de-la-Mer in the Camargue. The delicious, fruity olive oil that is so important in such a simple recipe comes from Maître Cornille's mill at Maussane. 'Cooking loup in this way is not really cuisine,' Monsieur Dumas said modestly, 'but if you've eaten it like this once, you'll never want to have it any other way.'

SEAWEED (IF AVAILABLE) *
1½–1¾ LB/700–800 G SEA BASS
    FILLETS
COARSE SEA SALT & BLACK PEPPER
16 ORANGE SEGMENTS, PEELED
8 LEMON SEGMENTS, PEELED
5–6 TBSP/75–90 ML OLIVE OIL

* If you do not have access either to a large

enough steamer or fish kettle, you can cook the fillets in foil with a little lemon juice, butter, salt & pepper. Put them on a baking tray in an oven pre-heated to 400°F/200°C/gas 6 and allow 9–10 minutes for a 7 oz/ 200 g fillet.

Pack the seaweed in a steamer big enough to hold the fish in a single layer, and bring (continued on next page) about 1 in/2.5 cm of water to the boil in the bottom. Add the fish, sprinkle with salt & cover tightly. In the meantime gently heat (but do not fry) the oranges and lemons in the olive oil. As soon as the fish is cooked, transfer to heated plates, pour over the citrus compote, grind on a little pepper and serve with plain, softly boiled rice.

· BROUFFADO des · MARINIERS du RHÔNE
Rhône ferrymen's stew (6)

This very old recipe for marinated beef cooked with anchovies, a simpler version of one that Monsieur Dumas serves, is known up the Rhône river as far as Lyons. The river ferrymen used to carry it in big pots ready to heat up in the evening and it is still a dish that is better on the second day than the first.

3 LB/1.4 KG LEAN BEEF SUCH AS
    CHUCK OR TOPSIDE/ROUND, CUT
    IN 12 SLICES

· MARINADE ·

2 TBSP/30 ML OLIVE OIL

2 TBSP/30 ML RED WINE VINEGAR

1 3 IN/7.5 CM STRIP DRIED
    ORANGE ZEST

1 BAY LEAF

6 CLOVES

SALT & PEPPER

¼ TSP/1.25 ML NUTMEG

OLIVE OIL

1 BIG ONION, FINELY CHOPPED

2 GARLIC CLOVES, PEELED AND
    FINELY CHOPPED

3 TBSP/45 ML CAPERS

· SAUCE ·

6 ANCHOVIES, SOAKED IN MILK

1 CLOVE GARLIC

1 TSP/5 ML OLIVE OIL

3–4 TSP/15–17.5 ML CORNICHONS
    (GHERKINS), CHOPPED, FOR
    GARNISH

Cover the beef with marinade, rub it in well and leave overnight. The next day oil a flameproof casserole (just big enough to hold all the ingredients closely packed) and in it layer the beef, onion, garlic and capers. Pour the marinade over the top, press down very well & seal hermetically, leaving as little room as possible between the meat and the cover. Cook in a low oven or over a low flame for 3 hours. Just before the end of cooking, pound the anchovies with 1 clove of garlic and 1 tsp/5 ml of olive oil. Beat into this half a glass of warm water, to form a thick paste. When the meat is cooked, lift onto a warmed serving plate, strain the juice and beat it together with the anchovy mixture. Let this simmer for a couple of minutes and then spoon it over the meat. Serve with a little mound of cornichons in the centre of each slice.

On the winelist at Vaccarès is the remarkable Coteaux des Baux DOMAINE DE TRÉVALLON, from a vineyard that has been carved out of the rocky hills of Les Alpilles by Eloi Dürrbach.

·ARLES MARKET·

On Saturdays Arles market reveals more than just its Provençal origins; not only Arles sausages are sold, but also the furry-looking strips of dried salt cod or morue, 'Morue pour la Brandade', as some of the stalls advertise. Brandade de morue is a creamy blend of salt cod, warm milk & olive oil famous in the Languedoc region as well as in south-west Provence. The name is said to come from the French word to brandish, which is what cooks, before the electric blender, used to have to do with their wooden spoons in order to make the laborious dish. In Provence it is often used in puff pastry tarts or to fill fresh ravioli pasta.

· MORUE à la PROVENCALE ·
gratin of salt cod (4)

Brandade de morue, with its high proportion of oil & milk (about 8 fl oz/¼ litre oil & 8 fl oz/ ¼ litre milk beaten into every 2 lb/1 kg of salt cod), can sit heavily on uninitiated stomachs. This 19th-century dish of cod gratinéd with fresh lemon & sweet red pepper is a lighter alternative.

1 LB/500 G (BEFORE SOAKING) DRIED
  SALT COD
6 LEEKS, TRIMMED & SLICED
  LENGTHWISE
2 SHALLOTS, FINELY CHOPPED
1 CLOVE GARLIC, FINELY CHOPPED
2–3 TBSP/30–45 ML OLIVE OIL
3 TBSP/45 ML CHOPPED FRESH PARSLEY
1 LARGE RED PEPPER, CORED &
  SLICED
FRESHLY GROUND BLACK PEPPER
1 LEMON, PEELED & FINELY SLICED
FINE BREADCRUMBS

First prepare salt cod: soak it in cold water (changing the water frequently) for 24–36 hrs. Drain, cover with more cold water and cook briskly below boiling point – salt cod must never boil – for 8–10 mins, until just tender. (This is the point when the cod would be used for Aïoli or Brandade.) Preheat the oven to 175°C/ 350°F/gas 4. Drain the cod very well, skin and bone it. Cook the leeks, shallots and garlic in a little oil and, when softened, mix with the parsley, red peppers & lots of black pepper. Pour half this mixture into an oiled, ovenproof casserole. On top lay half the lemon slices, cod, the remaining lemon and the rest of the leek mixture. Cover in fine breadcrumbs, drizzle over some oil and bake for 1 hour, turning the heat up for the last 10 mins to brown the top.

*M*editerranean people have always liked the taste of anise: Greeks drink it as ouzo in the shade of the Parthenon, in Beirut they quaff gulps of raki, in Naples sambucca, & in Marseilles pastis. Absinthe was once the preferred anise drink until, by 1915, it had so ravaged the French population that it was prohibited; & because of its strong taste of anise, incorrectly presumed to be toxic, all other anise drinks were banned as well.

*T*his didn't stop bar owners in Marseilles who went on serving their own home-brewed anise drinks. Just before 1932, when French authorities finally made the commercial production of pastis officially legal, a 23-year-old Marseilles painter was told by his father, 'Paul, you've got to get a proper job – this painting business is not for the son of a middle-class wine-dealer.' The young painter was Paul Ricard – whose blend of Provençal herbs, anise, sugar & natural alcohol is now the most famous aperitif in France.

*I*n 1974 it was discovered that Ricard pastis tasted as good, or better, when home-grown Camargue fennel was substituted for the original & costly Chinese star anise. Now the Camargue's fennel fields are as familiar as its black bulls, white horses & flamingoes.

LES SEICHES à la CAMARGUAISE
cuttlefish cooked in pastis Camargue style (4)

The best way to eat the tiny cuttlefish called 'petits supions' in Provence is as they do in what was once the cowboys' hunting lodge, the Hostellerie de Méjanes, on the Ricard ranch at Méjanes. The chef there, Monsieur Portas (also an expert in the cooking of whole bulls), cleans them, rolls them in seasoned flour & fries them crisply in good olive oil. With a cold glass of pastis (or several) & the fresh licorice smell of the nearby fennel fields, it makes a good break from flamingo spotting. An alter-native is to throw the pastis into the pan with the cuttlefish & let them absorb it as they cook.

1 LB 6 OZ/625 G CUTTLEFISH,
  CLEANED OF BONE AND INK SAC
9 FL OZ/250 ML LIGHT STOCK
6 FL OZ/165 ML DRY WHITE WINE
OLIVE OIL
2 GARLIC CLOVES, CRUSHED
SALT & PEPPER
HANDFUL FRESH PARSLEY,
  ROUGHLY CHOPPED
1 SHALLOT OR SMALL ONION,
  FINELY CHOPPED
6 OZ/175 G FRESH SPINACH,
  WASHED WELL & SHREDDED
1 SMALL LIQUEUR GLASS PASTIS

Slice cuttlefish so that the legs come away all together and the heads in ½. Bring stock, wine, 2 tbsp/30 ml of olive oil, garlic, 1 tsp/5 ml salt & parsley to a boil, add cuttlefish & enough boiling water to cover. Simmer covered, over medium heat for 20–25 minutes. Then put a little oil in a large, heavy-based frying pan & soften shallot or onion in it. Add spinach, stir once or twice, & then add the cuttlefish. Pour over the pastis, & enough of the cooking liquid just to barely cover. Season with salt & pepper & let simmer, uncovered, over low heat for 20 minutes, adding tablespoons of cooking liquid as needed. Serve with a dollop of aïoli in the middle or with a bowl of creamy saffroned rice.

· MOULES au PASTIS ·
mussels cooked in pastis (4)

This recipe is also good for tellines, but be sure to soak them overnight in fresh cold water to get rid of sand.

4 PINT (4 LB)/2 KG MUSSELS, BEARDS
    REMOVED & CLEANED OF SEAWEED

2 SHALLOTS OR 1 SMALL ONION,
    FINELY CHOPPED

2 GARLIC CLOVES, CRUSHED

10 FL OZ/300 ML DRY WHITE WINE

5 FL OZ/150 ML PASTIS

1 TSP/5 ML CORIANDER SEEDS

3 TINNED (OR VERY GOOD FRESH)
    TOMATOES, CRUSHED OR

3–4 TBSP/45–60 ML CRÈME
    FRAÎCHE OR DOUBLE/HEAVY
    CREAM

6 TBSP/90 ML OLIVE OIL

HANDFUL FRESH PARSLEY,
    CHOPPED

SALT & PEPPER

Soak mussels for 20 mins in a couple of changes of fresh cold water & discard any with damaged shells or that are much heavier than others. Bring shallots, garlic, wine, pastis, coriander, tomatoes (if you are not using cream) & olive oil to a full boil. When reduced by ½, throw in mussels & parsley, cover tightly & shake pan for 5–10 mins over a high flame until most mussels have opened. Remove mussels to very hot serving bowls. Stir the cream, pepper & salt (if needed) into the sauce. When this has heated through pour it over the mussels & serve immediately with plenty of crusty bread or garlic-rubbed toast.

A GRAND AÏOLI IN ST RÉMY

4½ LB/2 KG SALT COD
5 SMALL ARTICHOKES
12 CARROTS
1 MEDIUM BEETROOT
1 LB/500 G GREEN BEANS
1 LB/500 G CHICKPEAS
20 SMALL POTATOES
3 DOZEN SNAILS
10 BIG MUSHROOMS
10 STICKS OF CELERY
2 DOZEN BLACK OLIVES
SEVERAL HEADS OF FENNEL
AÏOLI OF 8 EGGS, 20 CLOVES
    OF GARLIC & OLIVE OIL
(ENOUGH FOR 10 PEOPLE)

Truffle hunting in the
LUBÉRON

*N*orth of
Aix-en-Provence
rises the long, blue
mass of the Lubéron moun-
tain. Some historians believe that the name comes from the
Provençal word for rabbit, supposedly referring to the
mountain's shape. It would need a good stretch of the
imagination to see any resemblance, but the Lubéron people
have certainly roasted a lot of 'lapin' in their time, so
perhaps the name is not unjustified.

*T*he Lubéron foothills, the Petit Lubéron, are topped with
a series of stone villages, originally built to offer refuge
from Saracen marauders in the ninth century. They continued to provide protection from later marauders throughout the Middle Ages and well into the nineteenth century,
when marauding became, if not less fashionable, at least
less violent. Many of the villages were then abandoned to
become the ruins that today suggest etchings from a Sir
Walter Scott romance. Their former occupants moved to the
fertile fruit- and vegetable-rich valleys below to create what
is now the great market garden of France. More recent
marauders in Provence – artists, writers and muscians who
can afford to ignore agricultural inconvenience for the sake
of a view – have begun to restore the old villages to a semb-
lance of their past glory.

Truffes

*T*he villagers of the Lubéron may have left their hilltops to others but they still cling tenaciously to their old traditions. One of the most cherished is 'La Chasse' – hunting – and of all the game chased, the black truffle is one of the most revered. This dense, knobbly fungus, resembling nothing so much as the end result of a giant sheep's dinner, is a prize for which every Provençal worth the name reserves his poetry. Inauspicious to look at, and sometimes bland to the point of nonentity, the essence of a good truffle can even infiltrate an eggshell, endowing the resulting omelette with a heady perfume that transforms cynics into devoted admirers.

*A*bel Rivarel is a truffle admirer and hunter, supplying his friend Gabriel Rousselet (of the restaurant Les Bories in Gordes) with enough of the precious fungus to satisfy his customers. It has been a bad year for truffles so far – good for tourists, but too hot and dry for mushrooms – and Abel has had little success: 100 grams here, 200 grams there. Not like the winter of '59 when he found eight kilos in one day. Nor even 1978, the last great truffle year, when it rained for five months almost without stopping. That year the season lasted three months past its usual February peak. And every day, including Christmas, Abel walked the 5000 hectares of mountain that is considered his own personal truffle estate by the local people. It makes a lot of leg-work these days for a man in his 60s, but for Abel work is a pleasure, even in the bad years. He went to the seaside once: 'It was like anchovies in a tin – head to tail, head to tail.' He prefers his own wild hills, where the juniper, savory, thyme and rosemary grow so thickly on the ground that he and his dog Rita come home smelling of them.

*A*bel has walked over his country bush by bush, stone by stone, as his father and grandfather did before him, carrying a mysterious map of truffle hiding places in his memory. 'Under that tree in '59 I took two kilos ... this tree was good two years ago but no more — maybe in another three it will be good again.' The secret is to find the tell-tale circle of barren ground that slowly develops around any tree whose roots may now or in the future nurture truffles. Then Rita's tail begins to wag, while Abel points out likely patches to her. But hardly has she begun to rootle with nose and paws than he stops her. 'Doucement! How many times must I tell you to dig gently?' He finishes the digging with his hand and as the last clod of earth is freed from a golf ball-sized truffle its potent, fleshy scent is released, strong enough even for non-canine noses to appreciate.

Sometimes one of the wild boars whose tracks criss-cross the area gets to the truffles first, rooting up the ground greedily and ruining it for the future. Often, too, the fungus kills off the very tree that has nurtured it. Then all Abel's careful training of his dog, all his gently urging 'Cherche, Rita! Cherche!' is to no avail. He remembers just after the war when there was a surfeit of truffles – a friend used to bring back great sackfuls and discard all but the round ones. Abel grins, 'And this year I have barely enough to keep Gabriel happy – but who knows? Next year the harvest may be better ... or the year after that. Who knows?'

genièvre

'Abel et Rita'

91

·GORDES – LES BORIES·

*J*ust visible from
the startling red
ochre village of
Roussillon is Gordes,
perched dramatically on
a steep hillside and crowned
by a Rennaissance château. It
is a town of artists, mostly bad,
some good, lured there by the beauty of
its narrow streets and terraces of old stone houses.
West of the main Place du Marché is a smaller square filled with a
fountain, and a café called, for the moment, the Café Renaissance.
But presumably there has always been a café just there; it is the
ideal place to drink a glass of Côtes du Lubéron or iced Beaumes-de-
Venise, under a huge plane tree strung with lights, like Christmas
all year round.

*G*ordes is well known for a group of mysterious beehive-shaped
stone huts two miles south of the town. Some of these 'bories'
are thought to date from pre-Roman times and some from as
recently as the eighteenth century. For the last 25 years a group on
the hill above Gordes have housed 'Les Bories', one of the best restaurants in the Lubéron. At nearly 70, Gabriel Rousselet, its owner
and chef, still rises early to do his own shopping in the market at
Cavaillon. And his clever combination of regional specialities into
both new and traditional recipes is admired by everyone – even
Abel Rivarel, the truffle hunter, would prefer 'to eat like a king
once a month at Gabriel's' than pay less for something more
ordinary.

·CASSOULET du TRUFFES·
miniature truffle pie
to serve 1–2 as
an entrée

Monsieur Rousselet remembers
with nostalgia the days when
Gordes still celebrated its
October fête day by leading a
steer through the streets. Its fate?
To become 'une bonne daube de
boeuf' for the whole village,
served with a village-sized Tian
de Courge baked in the wood-
burning oven of the local boulangerie. This tradition has disap-
peared, but an older one
remains – the stalking and eating of truffles by local enthusiasts. Gabriel Rousselet bakes the
costly 'black pearls' in puff pastry with only the marginally less
princely wild cèpes as seasoning.

1 FRESH BLACK TRUFFLE,
  1–1½ OZ/25–40 G, SCRUBBED

1 OZ/25 G CHANTERELLES OR CEPS (OR
    CULTIVATED MUSHROOMS IF NEC-
    ESSARY), FINELY CHOPPED

SALT & PEPPER

1–2 TBSP/15–30 ML WARM WATER

½ OZ/10 G VERY GOOD UNSALTED BUTTER

2–3 OZ/50–75 G PUFF PASTRY

1 EGG, BEATEN

Preheat the oven to 450°F/230°C/
gas 8. Use an earthenware dish,
just big enough to hold the mushrooms, water and butter without
overflowing. Put the truffle in the
middle and surround with the
other mushrooms. Season,
sprinkle with water and dot with
butter. Roll out the puff pastry of
⅛ in/3 mm thickness, spread
over dish and seal the edges.
Brush with beaten egg and bake
for 20–25 mins until golden.
Serve immediately.

· GLACE à la LAVANDE ·
lavender praline
ice cream (1½ pints)

To the north-east of Gordes fields
of the world-renowned Provençal
lavender stretch like purple cor-
duroy across the hills. From the
flowers Monsieur Rousselet
makes this strange and fragrant
ice cream.

FOR THE PRALINE:

2 OZ/50 G CASTER SUGAR

½ OZ/13 G LAVENDER PETALS

FOR THE ICE CREAM:

½ PT/290 ML MILK

1 SPRIG OF LAVENDER (PLUS EXTRA
    TO DECORATE)

4 EGG YOLKS

2 OZ/50 G CASTER SUGAR

½ PT/290 ML DOUBLE/HEAVY CREAM,
    LIGHTLY WHIPPED

First, make the praline. Put the
sugar and lavender into a saucepan and melt over medium heat
until brown and caramellized.
Pour into a greased tray, cool
and then pound to a fine powder.
To make the ice cream, bring the
milk and lavender just to the
boil, remove from heat, cover
and leave to infuse for 30 mins
in a warm place. In the meantime beat together the egg yolks
and sugar until creamy. Remove
the lavender from the milk and
whisk the milk into the sugar
mixture. Heat slowly, stirring
constantly until the custard
coats the back of a wooden spoon.
Cool. Fold the whipped cream
gently and thoroughly into the
custard. Spoon into a deep freez-
ing container, cover and
freeze. When the ice cream is
half frozen stir in the praline
mixture, then re-freeze. Stir
well once more before the ice
cream sets hard. As lavender
only blooms in the
summer you may
wish to make
and freeze
a larger
quantity
of this.

lavande ~trouvée
juillet '86

· APT AND MÉNERBES ·

In an article entitled 'Excursion Gastronomique – Midi de la France' written for a journal, Le Gastronome, in 1839, a certain Monsieur Fortuné Pin commends his home town of Apt for its excellent glacé fruits – apricots, quinces and melons – its cheeses and butters tasting of hazelnuts, its turkeys fattened on acorns, and its truffles 'as famous for their aroma as those of the Périgord and better for preserving'.

· GÂTEAU aux RAISINS · et FRUITS CONFITS d'APT
grape cake with glacé fruit from Apt

The glacé fruit from Apt is now more commercialized than in Monsieur Pin's day, and not so precious as that from Nice's Auer shop. It is better used to decorate baked goods, as in this moist fruitcake from the lovely Lubéron town of Ménerbes.

7 OZ/200 G MUSCAT GRAPES OR
   BLACK CHERRIES (STONED/
   PITTED)

RUM

7 OZ/200 G PLAIN WHITE FLOUR

PINCH OF SALT

2 LEVEL TSP/10 ML BAKING
   POWDER

5 OZ/150 G CASTER SUGAR

5 FL OZ/150 ML OLIVE OIL

2 TSP/10 ML VANILLA EXTRACT

2 EGGS

2 TBSP/30 ML MILK

SLICED (NOT DICED) GLACÉ
   FRUIT FOR DECORATION

Put the grapes and rum in a bowl and leave for 1 hour to marinate. Preheat the oven to 350°F/180°C/gas 4. Grease a 7–8 in/18–20 cm round cake tin and line with oiled greaseproof paper. Sift together the flour, salt and baking powder in a bowl. Beat the sugar, oil and vanilla together until light and smooth. Add the eggs one at a time, beating each time. Fold in the sifted dry ingredients and milk. Remove the grapes from the rum, roll lightly in flour and stir into the cake mixture. Pour into the cake tin, level the surface and decorate with glacé fruits. Bake in the centre of the oven until a knife inserted in the centre comes out dry – about 1¼ hours. Turn out of the pan when lukewarm and cool on a wire rack.

Serve with chilled Beaumes-de-Venise.

· VIENS ·

*F*rom *Viens, just west of Apt, you can see the Alps, even on a misty day. Cliffs drop sheer from the east walls of this tiny medieval village to a valley that marks the border between the Vaucluse district and the mountains of Haute Provence. And although Viens is no more than 20 kilometres from the luscious vegetable market at Apt, the cooking of its auberge Chez Bouquet has its roots in the rough and warming country food of the Provençal Alps. Madame Aline Bouquet and her daughter Pascale continue the tradition of 'cuisine famili- ale' that began when Monsieur Bouquet's mother was patronne. 'Don't call it haute cuisine,' said Paul Bouquet, 'it's just good home cooking.'*

*T*he *day that Monsieur Bouquet talked about his cuisine, or lack of it, a gipsy circus was being set up 100 yards from the restaurant: their goats were tethered just out- side and a guest's dog occasionally let out deep rumbling growls as the smell of caged tigers drifted down the hill. Chez Bouquet is more like a friend's kitchen than a restaurant dining room; lace curtains blow against a huge old wooden sideboard on which rest family dishes, jars of preserved vegetables and brandied cherries, bowls of local honey and baskets of cheese; a village woman stops by, baby on hip, to get Aline's old recipe for wild hare pâté and Monsieur Bouquet moves from table to table telling stories & exchanging a bottle of wine for a jug of water a guest has received by mistake. 'Here even the water tastes like wine!'*

95

· LÉGUMES à l'HUILE ·
fresh vegetables in olive oil

The local wild mushroom called 'tête de nègre' is a huge, black-capped cèpe (cep or Boletus) that the Bouquets consider superior to the more famous cèpe de Bordeaux. Their method of preserving it, to serve through the winter months as a luscious hors d'oeuvre, works very well with aubergines/eggplant or sweet peppers instead.

1 ONION, FINELY CHOPPED

1 CARROT, FINELY CHOPPED

3 CLOVES GARLIC, CRUSHED

PLENTY OF GOOD OLIVE OIL

SALT & PEPPER

15 FL OZ/400 ML WHITE WINE
   VINEGAR

15 FL OZ/400 ML WATER

BUNCH OF FRESH HERBS, TIED
   (THYME, ROSEMARY, MARJORAM)

5–6 CORIANDER SEEDS

10–12 WHOLE PEPPERCORNS

2 LB/1 KG WILD MUSHROOMS,
   CLEANED & SLICED
   LENGTHWISE <u>OR</u>

MIXED SMALL RED & GREEN
   PEPPERS, CORED & SLICED
   LENGTHWISE <u>OR</u>

AUBERGINES/EGGPLANT,
   TRIMMED, HALVED AND
   SLICED LENGTHWISE

4 BAY LEAVES

A FEW SPRIGS OF THYME

First make a marinade by cooking the onion, carrot and garlic in a little oil until softened. Season with salt & pepper and add the vinegar, water, the bunch of herbs, coriander & peppercorns. Boil for 10 minutes. Chill the vegetables overnight in the stock, drain and put in one or more preserving jars. Push the bay leaves and thyme down the sides, cover with olive oil and put on the lid. Store for 1 month before tasting. Serve with thin crisp toast to absorb the fragrant juices.*

· TERRAÏETO ·
little country pâtés

Terraïeto are tiny terracotta pots, almost as small as dollhouse china, into which are pressed a collection of different country pâtés: thrush, chicken liver, wild hare or rabbit.

2 GARLIC CLOVES, CRUSHED

1 ONION, FINELY CHOPPED

OLIVE OIL

2 RABBIT LIVERS (OR 12 CHICKEN)

2 LAMB'S KIDNEYS

1 TBSP/15 ML EACH OF CHOPPED
   PARSLEY & THYME

3 EGGS, BEATEN

SALT & BLACK PEPPER

9 FL OZ/250 ML TOMATO COULIS

1 SLICE OF BREAD, SOAKED IN
   BOUILLON

SMALL GLASS EAU DE VIE

Preheat oven to 375°F/190°C/gas 5. Cook garlic & onions in olive oil until soft. Add liver & kidneys & continue cooking for 3 mins. Chop finely & mix with other ingredients. Press into several small ovenproof dishes & cook for 45 minutes. Serve warm or cool.

· TIAN de COURGE ·
pumpkin gratin (6)

On wintry Sundays there is
always a roast on the Bouquets'
fireplace spit. The vegetables
may be whole onions baked in
richly herbed meat juices or a
terracotta dish may appear,
filled with this melting tian
of pumpkin. 'Tian' refers both
to a Provençal gratin & also
to the dish in which it is
cooked. Before gas and electric ovens made their appearance, the tian, with sunken
coal-filled metal lid, was
placed on a three-footed
iron stand in the
corner of the
fireplace.

2 LB/1 KG PUMPKIN, PEELED,
SEEDED & CHOPPED IN
SMALL CUBES

½ CUP RICE, BOILED FOR
10 MINUTES & DRAINED WELL

1 HANDFUL GRATED GRUYÈRE
CHEESE

4 TBSP/60 ML FLOUR, SIEVED

3 CLOVES GARLIC, FINELY
CHOPPED

5 TBSP/75 ML THYME, FINELY
CHOPPED

½ TSP/2.5 ML FRESHLY GRATED
NUTMEG

SALT & PEPPER

4 OZ/100 G BREADCRUMBS
(OPTIONAL)

OLIVE OIL

Preheat the oven to 325°F/ 170°C/gas 3. Toss together all the ingredients except bread-crumbs until pumpkin is well covered with flour and herbs. Put into a well-oiled gratin dish and cover with bread-crumbs. Drizzle a few tbsp of olive oil over the top and bake until top is crusty and deep caramel brown. The pumpkin will have an almost purée-like consistency. It is excellent either on its own with a crisp winter salad or as an accompaniment to a simple roast.

· TIAN de COURGE SUCRÉE ·
sweet pumpkin pudding

The art of good cooking is to make the most of a few simple ingredients. In Provence this means that many vegetables such as pumpkins, courgettes/ zucchini and spinach are used in both sweet & salted dishes with equally delicious results. The baked pumpkin in this recipe, with its spices & crunchy caramellized topping, has similarities with the filling of American pumpkin pie.

2 LB/1 KG PUMPKIN, PEELED, DE-SEEDED & CHOPPED IN SMALL CUBES
3 OZ/70 G BUTTER
3 OZ/70 G SUGAR
½ TSP/2.5 ML CINNAMON
½ TSP/2.5 ML NUTMEG, FRESHLY GRATED
2 TBSP/30 ML ORANGE PEEL, FINELY GRATED
4 OZ/100 G GRUYÈRE, GRATED (OPTIONAL)
5 EGGS, BEATEN
1 SMALL GLASS RUM (OPTIONAL)
4 OZ/100 G BREADCRUMBS MIXED WITH:
2 TBSP/30 ML SUGAR

Preheat the oven to 450°F/ 230°C/gas 8. Cook the pumpkin, covered, for about 15 mins in very little water. When tender, drain and purée. Melt half the butter in a frying pan, add the sugar & pumpkin and cook for about 10 minutes. Mix in the spices, orange peel & cheese. Remove from heat and when cool, fold in eggs & rum, if used. Pour mixture into a but-tered serving dish, press breadcrumbs & sugar into the top, dot with remaining butter and bake until the top is crunchy & brown. Serve warm.

*F*rom Apt the road south climbs past vineyards into the Lubéron's rugged core, dropping suddenly to a narrow river gorge that snakes through the mountains to Lourmarin, where Albert Camus is buried. Overshadowing the town, at least in size, is a massive fifteenth-century château to the west. Denise Pélas lives down the road from the château, next to a farmhouse in which both her father and grandmother were born, grew up and worked. Denise was smitten when young by the tastes and smells of her paternal grandmother's cooking and even after years spent in other countries, those recipes are still the ones that she and her friends appreciate the most.

· BOEUF en DAUBE ·
Provençal beef stew (6–8)

The Provençal Daube is a stew, slow-cooked to tenderize the delicious but chewy beef that comes from the cattle of the Camargue, differing from other French beef stews in that it was originally made with water. Now, both ingredients and method may vary considerably from chef to chef. The Provençal poet Mistral was said to prefer the sauce finished off with anchovy. René Jouveau tells of the inn at Aix whose daube, made with a slice of dried orange peel, was so good that visitors would regularly forego dessert to eat three and even four helpings of it. Denise Pélas makes her daube, as did both her grandmother and the villagers at nearby Gordes, with beef marinated first in tarragon vinegar; it gives to the meat

and, if chilled, to the jelly a mysterious, delicately sharp taste.

4½ LB/2 KG GOOD STEWING BEEF (SUCH AS CHUCK STEAK) CUT IN 2 IN/5 CM SQUARES
TARRAGON VINEGAR TO SOAK, PLUS 3 TBSP/45 ML EXTRA
4–5 FRESH BAY LEAVES, OR 2–3 DRIED
5 CLOVES GARLIC, UNPEELED
COARSE SEA SALT; PEPPER
1 HANDFUL FINELY CHOPPED FRESH PARSLEY
1 CALF'S FOOT OR PIG'S TROTTER (OPTIONAL UNLESS DAUBE IS TO BE SERVED COLD EN GELÉE – SEE NOTE AT END OF RECIPE*)
7 OZ/200 G FRESH PORK FAT
1 ONION, FINELY SLICED
4–6 CARROTS, SLICED LENGTHWISE IN QUARTERS
STOCK JUST TO COVER
6 IN/15 CM STRIP ORANGE PEEL (OPTIONAL)

Roll each piece of beef well in vinegar and put into a lidded casserole with bay leaves and garlic. Sprinkle with salt, pepper, parsley and 3 tbsp/45 ml vinegar. Cover & leave to marinate for 12 hours in the refrigerator.

Blanch the calf's foot (if using) and cut into 4 pieces. When the beef has marinated, cut the pork fat in small pieces and melt in a heavy-based frying pan. Remove beef from marinade, pat dry, then brown on all sides in the fat over a high heat. Take out the beef with a slotted spoon, lower heat, add onion to pan & cook until golden. Then add the rest of the marinade (except garlic) and calf's foot. Cook for 10 minutes and then transfer, with beef & carrots, to a daubière or heavy-lidded flameproof casserole. Pour enough stock over to cover, add dried orange peel (if using) & cover closely. Cook over a very low heat or in a low oven for 5–7 hours.

(If using an earthenware daubière, cook in the oven, as direct contact with heat may crack it. If using a heavy cast iron casserole, oil some greaseproof paper, lay over the stew and seal hermetically with lid. The daube can then be cooked on top of stove over minimum heat. According to Denise, the surface of the daube should not bubble, but just move gently – the famous 'mijoter' of every French cook. It means, literally, 'to simmer' but also 'to cook lovingly', which is closer to the spirit of Provençal cooking.)

To serve the daube, skim off any excess fat and adjust seasoning. Strip the meat from the calf's foot, add to the daube and discard the bones. Ladle some of the juice from the meat over a bowl of hot macaroni on which you have grated a handful of Gruyère and bring both daube and macaroni to the table.

Chefs in Avignon add four cloves to the marinade & then cook it with twelve walnuts, quartered & toasted.

To serve a daube as Mistral liked it, purée 2 anchovies and mix with the cooking juices before end of simmering.

TO SERVE THE PREVIOUS RECIPE EN GELÉE, AS A COLD SUMMER DISH: omit the stock & extra vinegar & add 1¾ pt/1 litre of red wine to the marinade. Make sure the meat is just covered with liquid during cooking & sealed well to keep mois-ture in. When the daube has finished cooking, discard the calf's foot/pig's trotter, arrange the meat & vegetables decoratively in a terrine (deep enough to hold juice as well) and strain juice over top. Refrigerate until set (4–5 hours) & skim fat which has risen to the surface. Remove jellied daube from terrine by dipping the base briefly in hot water, then inverting terrine over serving dish. Press finely chopped fresh parsley into the meat & serve with grain mustard, olives & cornichons (gherkins/pickles).

· POULE ·
aux OLIVES VERTES
chicken with green olives (6)

If many of Denise's recipes seem to be slow-cooked ones, there is a good reason. They date from the days *when her family worked in the vineyards picking grapes, & these one-pot dishes could be left by the fire all day, to simmer gently & imbibe the perfumes of wine & herbs.*

4½ LB/2 KG BOILING FOWL

SALT & PEPPER

OLIVE OIL

1 MEDIUM ONION, FINELY
   CHOPPED

2 TBSP/30 ML COGNAC

1 BOTTLE WHITE WINE (NOT
   TOO ACID)

2 TBSP/30 ML EACH CHOPPED
   FRESH THYME, MARJORAM &
   SAVORY OR 1 TSP/2.5 ML EACH
   OF DRIED HERBS

2 MEDIUM TOMATOES, PEELED,
   DE-SEEDED & ROUGHLY CHOPPED
   (OR TINNED TOMATOES IF
   FRESH ONES ARE NOT TASTY)

6 OZ/175 G MUSHROOMS (OR DRIED
   CEPS SOAKED IN WARM WATER)

6 OZ/175 G GREEN OLIVES, STONED/
   PITTED & RINSED WELL IN
   COLD WATER

GARLIC CROÛTONS TO GARNISH:

3 CLOVES GARLIC, PEELED
   AND CRUSHED

3 TBSP OLIVE OIL

½ A SMALL FRENCH BREAD
   LOAF, CUT IN THIN SLICES

4 TBSP FRESH PARSLEY,
   FINELY CHOPPED

Cut the chicken in 6 pieces, season with salt & pepper & brown on all sides in oil in a heavy-based frying pan. Lower the heat and add the onion, cooking until pale golden. Pour the cognac over the chicken, light it, and when the flame dies down, transfer everything to a large flameproof marmite or casserole. Add wine, herbs & tomatoes. Wine should just cover the chicken. Cover and cook over a low heat until chicken is tender (about 2½ hours).

In the meantime make the garlic croûtons. Leave the garlic in the olive oil for about 1 hour. Then dip a pastry brush into the oil & brush across both sides of each slice of bread. Grill bread until brown & then toss in parsley. (The croûtons can be used to garnish stews, soups & salads.)

15 minutes before the chicken has finished cooking, sauté mushrooms for 3 mins in a little oil, then transfer them with juices to casserole. Cook uncovered for rest of time to reduce slightly. When cooked, remove chicken & mushrooms & keep warm on serving dish. Skim fat from sauce and strain it into a small saucepan. Bring to the boil, turn down heat, add olives & simmer for 5 mins. Adjust seasoning, spoon sauces & olives over chicken & scatter hot homemade croûtons on top.

· AUBERGINES aux TOMATES ·
aubergines/eggplant with tomato sauce (4)

In Provence they say that aubergines are 'gourmandes' because they eat too much oil. Denise's secret is to use lots of oil, rather than a little, but very, very hot. In this way the surface of the aubergines seals quickly and the resulting dish is rich but not oily.

2 LB/1 KG AUBERGINES/EGGPLANT,
   CUT INTO $\frac{1}{2}$ IN/1 CM CUBES

OLIVE OIL

2 LB/1 KG GOOD FRESH TOMATOES,
   DE-SEEDED, SKINNED AND
   ROUGHLY CHOPPED (OR EQUIVA-
   LENT WEIGHT TINNED)

3 CLOVES GARLIC, FINELY
   CHOPPED

HANDFUL FRESH PARSLEY,
   FINELY CHOPPED

3 TBSP/45 ML CHOPPED FRESH
   MARJORAM OR OREGANO

SALT & PEPPER

Heat the oil in a heavy frying pan until smoking & add the aubergines a handful at a time so as not to lower heat. Cook until golden (about 10 minutes) then remove with slotted spoon. Add tomatoes to pan with garlic, herbs & seasoning. Cook for 10 minutes, covered at first, then uncovered so that juice reduces by $\frac{1}{2}$. Return aubergines to pan to heat through – about 5 minutes.

· TIAN de ·
GRANDES COURGETTES
baked marrows/giant zucchini (4)

The Lourmarin market people save giant zucchini or marrows for Denise. Most cooks prefer the smallest size but Denise feels that if excess liquid is allowed to evaporate, the larger vegetables have a more intense taste.

1 ONION, FINELY CHOPPED

OLIVE OIL

1 MARROW/GIANT ZUCCHINI, CUT
   IN ROUNDS (ABOUT 2 LB/1 KG)

2 BAY LEAVES

SALT & FRESHLY GROUND PEPPER

4 TBSP/60 ML FLOUR

4 TBSP/60 ML CHOPPED PARSLEY

4 OZ/120 G GRUYÈRE CHEESE,
   GRATED

4 TBSP/60 ML BUTTER

Preheat the oven to 425°F/ 220°C/gas 7. Sauté onion in oil until soft. Add marrow, bay leaves, salt & pepper. Cover & cook over a high heat for 5 minutes. Remove lid, lower heat to medium & cook until juice evaporates. Test seasoning. Dust top of marrow with flour and parsley and cover surface with Gruyère. Dot with small pieces of butter and bake for $\frac{1}{2}$ an hour.

Often only one dish is memorable in a meal, and even a bowl of wrinkled purplish-black olives is improved by the warmth of sun through leafy branches, or by the enthusiasm of a friendly waiter. Asked why he believed the old-fashioned Provençal cuisine was so good, a waiter in the hilltop town of Bonnieux said, 'Madame, nowadays we bathe in the sun. In my grandmother's day, they ate it.'

· TRUFFES de CHÈVRE · en TAPENADE
goat cheese truffles in olive pâté (4)

Some foods, olives in particular, taste of the sun; tapenade, the pungent olive pâté made with crushed anchovies and capers, tastes unforgettably of Provence. It can inspire passionate devotion and equally passionate aversion. At the restaurant César in Bonnieux, tapenade is turned into another oddly interesting dish: tiny fresh chèvres (goat cheeses), no bigger than 1½ in/4 cm in diameter, are rolled in the black olive pâté to give the appearance of whole truffles, then served on a salad of bitter radicchio & curly endive. Because this combination of cheese & olives is very rich, the salad should be dressed with less oil than usual.

FOR THE TAPENADE:

11 OZ/300 G STONED/PITTED BLACK OLIVES

7 OZ/200 G RINSED CAPERS

2 ANCHOVIES, RINSED IN MILK TO REMOVE SALT

1 CLOVE GARLIC, CRUSHED

1 TSP/5 ML WHOLE GRAIN MUSTARD OR PEPPER

1 FRESH BAY LEAF, FINELY CHOPPED

HANDFUL FRESH THYME, LEAVES FINELY CHOPPED

1 SMALL GLASS COGNAC

2 TSP/10 ML LEMON JUICE

OLIVE OIL

4–8 SMALL GOAT CHEESES (OR SOFT FRESH CHÈVRE ROLLED INTO SMALL BALLS)

1 SMALL HEAD RADICCHIO

1 SMALL HEAD CURLY ENDIVE

Pound together (or blend to achieve a coarse pâté) the solid ingredients. Stir in the cognac & lemon juice, then beat in olive oil, drop by drop until the consistency is of thick jam. Roll each cheese in the tapenade to cover completely & serve on a salad with thin crisp toast.

·OPPÈDE – SIMONE BONNET·

*S*imone Bonnet lives in an old Lubéron windmill surrounded by fruit trees and vineyards. Her ancient Citroën is battered from carrying kilos of grapes to market and from the regular barrage of figs, cherries & walnuts that fall from the trees onto it. Simone's family is the oldest in Oppède, a relatively modern town that sits below the impossibly pictur-esque mountain-top ruin of Oppède-le-Vieux. Her 90-year-old Aunt Julie is still an excellent cook: her pigeon aux lentilles is famous, as is the pork she roasts with whole garlic cloves cooked like flageolet beans in the pan juices. Aunt Julie remembers winters during the war when fresh vegetables were scarce; the family used aubergines & tomatoes sun-dried in the sum-mer & preserved in olive oil. Strings of orange peel & wild mushrooms were threaded with a needle and hung in the barn to dry, later to add their essential aroma to rich daubes and pot au feus.

· GIGOT d'AUBERGINES ·
aubergines/eggplant
baked liked roast lamb (6)

This aubergine dish is called a 'gigot' because it is baked whole in the same way as gigots of lamb – pricked all over with slices of garlic & roasted over charcoal. The same dish can easily be transformed into a peppery mousse (see below) & served with crusty bread.

---

3 AUBERGINES/EGGPLANT, WASHED
   AND PATTED DRY

6 CLOVES OF GARLIC, CUT
   LENGTHWISE IN SLIVERS

SPRIG FRESH MARJORAM, CHOPPED

SPRIG FRESH THYME, CHOPPED

OLIVE OIL

1–2 LEMONS FOR SERVING

Preheat the oven (if using) to 350°F/180°C/gas 4. Pierce the aubergines all over with a small sharp knife & press a sliver of garlic & a few herbs into each slit. Rub olive oil into the aubergine skins & either grill until black on a bar-becue or pack tightly into an oiled baking dish. Bake until tender (about 1 hour). Slice in half at the table & serve with a drizzle of olive oil & a lemon.

To serve as aubergine mousse: Ingredients as before plus nut-meg, salt & pepper.

Halve the cooked aubergines & scoop out the pulp into a bowl. Beat until creamy with several spoonfuls of olive oil, a pinch of nutmeg & a squeeze of lemon. Season with salt & black pepper.

·GÂTEAU de FRUITS BATTUS·
broken fruit pudding

In France's Limousin region, cooks made this baked pudding with black cherries. In Provence, it is often made with muscat grapes & scented with fragrant Beaumes-de-Venise wine. Simone's Aunt Julie wouldn't call it a recipe, 'It's just to use up broken, over-ripe fruit.'

1½ LB/700 G MUSCAT GRAPES, WASHED & DRIED

2 OZ/60 G FLOUR, SIFTED WITH A PINCH OF SALT

2 OZ/60 G SUGAR

½ TSP/2.5 ML NUTMEG

4 EGGS

1 PT/600 ML MILK

4 TBSP/6 ML BEAUMES-DE-VENISE WINE

Preheat the oven to 375°F/190°C/ gas 5. Place grapes in a well-buttered shallow baking dish. Mix together the flour, sugar & nutmeg & beat in the eggs one at a time, alternating with the milk. Stir in the wine & sieve the mixture over the grapes. Bake until brown & puffed up (about 45 minutes), dust with sugar & serve luke-warm with a jug of cream.

· CONSERVE du SOLEIL ·
cherries preserved in brandy

Simone's shelves are lined with jars of whole cherries, apricots, plums and homemade herbal eaux-de-vie. This recipe for bran-died cherries is called 'Conserve du Soleil' because she leaves the fruit in the sun's warmth for at least 40 days.

STEP 1:

1½ LB/750 G SWEET BLACK CHERRIES

1¾ PT/1 LITRE 40° PROOF FRUIT ALCOHOL, POLISH PURE SPIRITS, PLAIN EAU-DE-VIE OR BRANDY

1 VANILLA POD

2 CLOVES

1 CINNAMON STICK

STEP 2:

1½ LB/750 G BITTER CHERRIES

11 OZ/300 G SUGAR

Give each sweet black cherry a tap with a mallet so that the skin splits, being careful not to crush the fruit completely. Put into a large, sterilized glass jar with the alcohol and spices, seal very tightly and leave for 15–20 days. Then filter the mixture & pour into 2 sterilized 2 lb/1 kg preserving jars with the bitter cherries, whose stems must

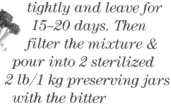

be trimmed, and the
sugar. Seal and leave in a sunny
place if possible, for at least
two months before tasting.
Serve the brandy in small
glasses with a spoon for the
cherries.

· CABRIÈRES D'AVIGNON ·

*A*fter the hilltop roller-coaster ride of Oppède, Ménerbes, Bonnieux, Roussillon and Gordes, the country settles down into a wide, peaceful valley with towns that are more practical, if less like etchings from eighteenth-century romances. At Cabrières-d'Avignon, near the lovely watery town of L'Isle-sur-la-Sorgue, Michel Bosc and his family have a café where villagers come to discuss the relative merits of the year's Côtes du Lubéron. Michel Bosc's parents worked as bakers and pastry-makers in the Bouches-du-Rhône area, where, in truffle and quince season, it was not uncommon for villagers to arrive mid-afternoon with one or both ingredients to have them wrapped in separate bundles of bread dough, and left in the oven, still warm from the morning's bread-baking, until supper. By then the truffles and quinces would have worked their magic on the little nests of bread, and the result, when they were cut open, was a burst of indescribable perfume.

TRUFFES à la CROQUE au SEL
· truffles baked in dough · with butter & salt

Sometimes it isn't a wine's bouquet that is discussed chez Bosc but, as happened one day in truffle season, the bouquet of a fresh truffle, sliced open and passed untasted from hand to hand and nose to nose. Colette, who lived and wrote in Provence, disdained all complications of the truffle's taste and all cooks who submerged the prized black fungus in glutinous masses of foie gras or in game and vegetables with heavy brown sauces. She would approve Michel's classic, simple recipe.

PER PERSON

2 TRUFFLES, 1 OZ/30 G EACH, CLEANED OR 2 GOOD WILD MUSHROOMS

12 OZ/350 G (APPROX) BREAD DOUGH (SEE RECIPE PAGE 111)

2 SMALL PATS UNSALTED BUTTER

½ TSP/2.5 ML COARSE SEA SALT

Preheat oven to 450°F/230°C/gas 8. Roll out dough to ½ in/1 cm thick. Wrap each truffle in dough and bake in hot oven until puffed up and golden brown. Split open at the table and let each person douse the truffles with butter and salt.

· PAN COUDON ·
quinces in pastry (4)

The delicate appley-pear taste of quinces is a nostalgic one for most Provençal people. The fruit are cooked for jellies and bonbons and also used to perfume the massive linen cupboards that were once part of every Provençal farmhouse. This recipe is an excellent way of enjoying cooked quinces (almost inedible when raw) and is good with apples too.

8 FL OZ/225 ML HONEY

8 OZ/225 G WALNUTS, ROUGHLY CHOPPED

6 QUINCES, CORED & PEELED, BUT WITH ½ IN/1 CM LEFT INTACT AT THE BOTTOM

1 LB/10 OZ/750 G SWEETENED BREAD OR FOUGASSE DOUGH (SEE RECIPE – PAGE 126)

1 EGG, BEATEN

CASTER SUGAR

Preheat the oven to 425°F/220°C/ gas 7. Melt the honey with the walnuts until the nuts begin to darken. Fill quinces with mixture. Roll out the dough to ½ in/1 cm thick and cut into 6 circles. In the middle of each, place a quince, wrap with dough and pinch firmly closed. You may want to make dough 'leaves' for decoration. Brush each dough-wrapped quince with beaten egg and bake for 25–30 mins. Sprinkle with caster sugar and serve hot with a jug of cream. Quinces or apples are also delicious filled with several spoonfuls of apricot conserve instead.

· PAIN aux OLIVES ·
olive bread
(2 loaves)

Cabrières-d'Avignon is lucky in having an old-fashioned baker who will still hand over a bit of bread dough in which to bake the occasional truffle or quince. He cooks a crusty, moist bread (served at the Bistrot à Michel) similar to this one filled with generous helpings of ripe black olives.

2 × 13 G SACHETS OF ACTIVE DRIED YEAST

2 LB/900 G FLOUR (A MIXTURE OF UNBLEACHED WHITE BREAD FLOUR WITH 2 GENEROUS HANDFULS OF BUCKWHEAT FLOUR, SIFTED)

APPROX 1 PT/500 ML TEPID WATER

2 TBSP/30 ML OLIVE OIL

1 LB/450 G BLACK OLIVES, STONED AND CRUSHED

Stir together the yeast and a handful of flour in enough water to make a runny batter. Leave for 1 hour. Warm the remaining flour slightly in the oven, mix in salt and make a well in the middle. Pour in the yeast mixture, adding enough tepid water to form a moist dough. Knead for 10–12 minutes on a lightly floured surface. Leave to rise in a large floured bowl covered with a dampened cloth. When the dough has doubled in size, turn out onto a floured work-surface, punch down and flatten it out. Sprinkle over the olive oil and work it thoroughly into the dough, kneading steadily for 10 minutes. Shape it into a ball and leave in the floured bowl, covered with a damp cloth until again nearly doubled in size. Preheat the oven to 450°F/230°C/ gas 8. Divide the dough in half and on a floured board roll each half into a rectangle. (continued on following page)

111

Spread these with the olives, roll up and leave the surface to dry slightly. Brush with water, slip the loaves onto a heated metal baking sheet and place in the oven. After 15 minutes turn the heat down to 375°F/190°C/gas 5 & continue baking for another 45 minutes – or until a knock on the bottom of the loaf produces a hollow sound. Cool on a wire rack.

Alphonse Daudet writes in his novel 'Tartarin' that the people of Tarascon liked the taste of spiced pears in baked dough.

· FOUGASSE aux GRATTONS ·
Provençal flat bread with crispy bacon
(2 loaves)

Grattons (sometimes spelt 'gratelons' in Provence) are little cripsly-fried pieces of rendered pork, used here to give this rich pastry the density of a salty short-bread.

· GRATTONS ·

1 LB 5 OZ/600 G BREAST OF PORK OR BELLY PORK, DICED

2 LB/900 G PORK FAT, DICED

10–12 TBSP/150–180 ML DRY WHITE WINE

• FOUGASSE •

½ BREAD DOUGH FROM PREVIOUS
  RECIPE

1 EGG YOLK, BEATEN

Cook the meat, fat and wine over a very gentle heat in a heavy covered saucepan. Press down on the meat several times during cooking to render up as much fat as possible. After 1½–2 hours, pour the liquid off through a strainer – it can be used instead of olive oil (and often was 50 years ago in Provence) for cooking. Crisp the diced meat over higher heat, straining off any liquid fat when necessary.

To make the fougasse, make the bread dough and after the first rising mix in the grattons: with a knife cut through the dough first one way and then the next. Reform into a ball and repeat. Gather the pieces together into a mass, divide in two and form into two flat loaves, slashed as on drawing of Fougasse aux gratelons, below. Spread the openings wide with your fingers so that they don't close up during baking. Brush the top with egg yolk and bake on a hot metal sheet for 30–35 minutes at 450°F/230°C/gas 8 until crisp and golden. Serve warm with a bitter salad such as endive or dandelion.

In both of these bread recipes, the crust will be much crisper if a pan of hot water is placed in the bottom of the oven during baking.

To rescue leftover crusts of good bread, brush each crust with olive oil top & bottom. Spread them with the tapenade sauce on page 105 or with good tomato coulis & add a few olives or anchovies (or a slice of tomato if you have used tapenade). Grill or cook in a hot oven until bubbling & serve with salad.

A PICNIC IN THE LUBÉRON

CAVAILLON MELON
TROUT & FRESH WATER CRAW-
  FISH FROM THE SORGUES R.
TRUFFLES FROM THE VAUCLUSE
MUSCAT GRAPES & CHERRIES
FRUIT CONFITURES
NOUGAT & GLACÉ FRUIT FROM
  APT
CÔTES DU LUBÉRON WINE

An Agreeable
BEVERAGE

I^{t is} October, and in the grape-rich countryside around
Avignon this year's harvest is nearly over. Only the
occasional near-collision is still caused by a farmer
trundling his tractor full of grapes down a narrow
country road, oblivious to oncoming traffic, speed-
limits and timetables – or indeed to any table but
the one in his own farmhouse kitchen. The wines of
this region are good ones: at the towns of Séguret,
Sablet and Vacquéras, there are robust Côtes du Rhône
Villages; at Gigondas the deep almost black-red
wines frequently rival all but the most outstanding
(but much more celebrated) Châteauneuf-du-Pape;
and west of Avignon both Lirac and Tavel produce
potent rosés. A bottle of Tavel may no longer cost
the sixpence it did in Tobias Smollett's days in
the late eighteenth century, but neither is it still
mixed with pigeon's dung and quick lime.

*B*y late October most of the foreign grape-harvesters –
students from America and even prostitutes from
Marseilles – have packed and left for the season, and the
cafés in Avignon, Orange and Vaison-la-Romaine are
no longer filled with northern ruin seekers. But
Paulette Antilogus still has a garden full of big nectar-
sweet tomatoes, on whose dense flesh the pink bloom
begins to fade as soon as they are picked. The same
flushed pink mixes with impossible yellows and flame
reds in the trees and vine leaves. It is a peaceful, sleepy

country, *years and worlds removed from the nearby city of Avignon.*

*T*he relative quiet of Avignon's old town is threatened on all sides by hideous suburbs, modern factories, high-rise tenements and the traffic that races to and from Paris and Marseilles on the autoroute; according to the signs, there is nowhere else to race from. Ramparts built in the fourteenth century, when Avignon was for 70 years the Papal seat, keep out some of the worst aspects of twentieth-century progress, but on market day the city is ringed with so many vehicles of every kind that they look like the covered wagons in old Westerns, gathered in a protective circle against attacking savages.

*A*vignon has bustled since 1309, when a French pope, John XXII, decided he couldn't put up with the crime and backstabbing of fourteenth-century Rome. He moved his pontifical court to the home country of his patron, the French King, Philippe the Fair. But the crime and backstabbing didn't seem to have noticeably diminished, if the poet Petrarch is to be believed. An Avignon lady, Laura, was the love of his life (though an unrelentingly virtuous love, married to someone else), yet he said *of her city '... money is adored ... Everything breathes lies: the air, the earth, the houses &, above all, the bedrooms ...'.*

*I*n spite of Petrarch's quibbles, the arrival of the popes heralded an unrivalled Golden Age for Avignon; the population grew, trade flourished & fine houses were built (as well as an astonishing number of brothels). Some idea of the city's change from provincial backwater to Papal residence can be grasped by reading the description of just one feast given to celebrate the coronation of Clement VI, the pope partially responsible for building Avignon's magnificent Palais des Papes: on May 19th 1344 the Brothers Précheur cooked: 118 steers, 1023 sheep, 101 calves, 914 goats, 60 pigs, 690 kg of lard & salt meat, 15 sturgeons & 11,971 mixed poultry. And 3250 eggs for the 50,000 pies.

*T*he wines for this feast must have come from nearby Châteauneuf-du-Pape, where in 1316 Clement VI's predecessor created '20 salmées of vines & olive groves'. To reach Châteauneuf & the other Côtes du Rhône wine towns from Avignon, you must first conquer the sign system. This has been designed to prevent strangers to the city from ever leaving it, or to lead determined escapees into the maze of country lanes to the east (which appear on no known maps, however large the scale) & there abandon them. The rewards are great, however, for those who do finally manoeuvre their way out of the Papal city: there can be no better introduction to the region than to sit in the town of Beaumes-de-Venise, at a table warm from the autumn sun, & to drink an aperitif of the town's amber wine, sweet with muscat grapes.

· ÉPICES PROVENÇALES ·
Provencal mixed spices

Despite propaganda claiming
the reverse, winter does
finally come to Provence & even
Provençal cooks must resort
to dried herbs for a change.
This old
mixed-
spice
recipe
brings
a strange but evocative taste of
the Provençal country to any
dish from aubergines to fish.
(All herbs weighed after drying.)

Grind to a powder in a mortar:
1 oz/25 g each thyme, serpolet
(wild thyme), savory, lavender,
rosemary, bay leaves, cloves,
orange peel, and 1 whole nutmeg. Mix well and store in
tightly-sealed bottles.
Use sparingly, as you
would dried
herbs.

·*LE CUISINIER MÉRIDIONAL*·

In 1835 an Avignon printer published 'Le Cuisinier Mérid-ional'. The introduction says, 'Only one other book about southern cuisine has been published, at a price too elevated for the common man. We publish here a book that can be used by everyone, with recipes culled from the most distinguished sources – even students of the celebrated Martel responded.' This 'celebrated Martel' was an Avignon traiteur/caterer, born in Tarascon in 1762, who had had a brilliant reputation as far away as Paris. When he died, in 1828, gastronomes mourned, fearing the demise of Avignon's culinary reputation. But Martel's students, notably a Monsieur Suau in Apt, con-tinued his tradition of fine cuisine, if not in Avignon, then at least in other Provençal towns. Suau was particularly renowned for his twelve 'petits pâtés à la Béchamelle', of which it was said: 'Better to have eaten this dish and lived for just one hour than continued another ten years without it.'

·*BEURRE de PROVENCE*· ou *AYOLI*
Provençal butter or Aïoli

Le Cuisinier Méridional gives an unusual but interesting recipe for aïoli, using Provence's sweet almonds instead of the usual quantity of egg yolks.

1 LARGE SLICE OF BREAD,
   TRIMMED OF CRUSTS & SOAKED
   IN TEPID WATER

2 GARLIC CLOVES, PEELED

6 LARGE ALMONDS,
   BLANCHED & PEELED

1 EGG YOLK

OLIVE OIL (APPROX 5–7 FL OZ/
   150–200 ML)

SALT & PEPPER (OPTIONAL)

Squeeze the bread out very well and remove the inside green sprouts from the garlic cloves. In a mortar pound the garlic, bread and almonds together to form a smooth paste. Beat in the egg yolk to give a creamier tex-ture, and then the oil, drop by drop (as for the aïoli on page 12). Stop when a smooth shining cream is formed and season with salt and pepper. Use when-ever a good mayonnaise is called for. This is especially good with poached, steamed or grilled fish such as salmon or trout.

· THON à la PROVENÇALE ·
SAUCE RÉMOULADE
Provençal tuna
with caper sauce (4)

Cut into thick fillets and
grilled over an open fire,
fresh tuna has a rich, meaty
flesh, long appreciated in
Provence. The first tuna,
fished off the coast between
Sète and Marseilles, rarely
appears before June – the
water is still too cold – and
the best time for it is
between September and
December.

· SAUCE RÉMOULADE ·

1 TSP/5 ML FRESH PARSLEY,
  FINELY CHOPPED

2 TBSP/30 ML CAPERS, WELL
  RINSED AND FINELY CHOPPED
  OR MASHED

1 TSP/5 ML ONION, PEELED AND
  FINELY CHOPPED

2 COOKED EGG YOLKS

2 ANCHOVY FILLETS, WELL
  RINSED

1 GARLIC CLOVE, PEELED AND
  CRUSHED (OPTIONAL)

1 RAW EGG YOLK

JUICE OF ½ LEMON OR
  TO TASTE

1 TUNA STEAK 1 IN/2.5 CM
  THICK OF ABOUT
  1¼ LB/500–600 G

4–5 TBSP/60–75 ML OLIVE OIL

1 BAY LEAF

2 TBSP/30 ML RED OR WHITE
  VINEGAR (TARRAGON IF
  POSSIBLE)

First make the sauce: pound
to a paste the parsley, capers,
onions, egg yolks, anchovies
and garlic (if using). Add the
raw egg yolk, then add the
olive oil, drop by drop, as for
aïoli, until you have a thick
paste. Season with as much
lemon juice as you like.

To prepare the fish, blanch it
first in boiling water and
remove the skin. Heat the
olive oil and bay leaf
together. Put in the tuna and
sprinkle with vinegar, turning it several times until it is
slightly browned on both
sides. Cover and simmer over
moderate heat for 30–45 minutes, until the tuna is flaky.
Drain well and serve with the
sauce rémoulade beside it.
You may also wish to add a
sliced onion at this point.

If you are cooking over a bar-
becue, marinate tuna in the
oil, vinegar and bay for 1–2
hours and then grill, brushing with the marinade, until
it begins to flake. Sauce
rémoulade is good with
almost all dry, meaty fish,
especially salmon.

· THON BRAISÉ ·
SAUCE POIVRADE
braised tuna in a
peppery sauce (4)

In the Cuisinier Méridional this recipe is given using sturgeon instead of tuna, with the note: 'All preparations for sturgeon are applicable equally to tuna.'

1 TUNA STEAK 1 IN/2.5 CM THICK
   OF ABOUT 1¼ LB/500–600 G
4 SMALL ONIONS, PEELED AND
   CUT IN SLICES
2 CARROTS, PEELED & SHREDDED
2 TURNIPS, PEELED & SHREDDED
3 TBSP/4–5 ML OLIVE OIL
1 LARGE BOUQUET GARNI
   (THYME, BAY, ROSEMARY)
SALT & PEPPER
9 FL OZ/250 ML WHITE WINE

· POIVRADE ·

2 ONIONS, PEELED & SLICED
2 CARROTS, CUT IN THIN SLICES
1 TURNIP, CUT IN THIN STRIPS
1 GARLIC CLOVE, PEELED AND
   CHOPPED
2 CLOVES
1 BAY LEAF
1 SPRIG OF THYME
2 TBSP/30 ML OIL OR BUTTER
PINCH OF FLOUR
1 WINEGLASS RED WINE
1 WINEGLASS WATER
1 TBSP/15 ML WINE VINEGAR
2 TBSP/300 ML TOMATO COULIS
   (SEE PAGE 35)
SALT & LOTS OF COARSELY
   GROUND BLACK PEPPER

Blanch and skin the tuna as in previous recipe. In a deep saucepan, large enough to hold all the ingredients, cook the onions, carrots and turnips in the oil until slightly softened. Add the bouquet garni, lay the tuna on top and sprinkle with salt, pepper and white wine. Cover and cook over moderately high flame for about 35–45 minutes until the tuna flakes.

In the meantime make the poivrade (which is a very versatile sauce and can be used to moisten everything from tame fish to wild duck). Cook the onions, carrots, turnip, garlic, cloves and herbs in the oil, just until beginning to turn golden. Add a pinch of flour and stir for a minute. Add the wine, water and vinegar and simmer for 30 minutes. Stir in the coulis, boil a further 10 minutes, skim off any fat and sieve. Season with salt and lots of freshly ground black pepper.

To serve the tuna, place on a large heated serving dish with the julienne of vegetables around it. Reduce the cooking liquid to a few tablespoons and stir in the poivrade. Pour over the tuna and serve immediately.

· CHÂTEAUNEUF-DU-PAPE ·

In 'Letres de mon Moulin' Alphonse Daudet wrote of the Avignon pope who, every Sunday after vespers, sat in the sun next to his mule and uncorked a bottle of wine: 'that excellent wine, the colour of rubies, that is called Châteauneuf-du-Pape'. The wine is now world-famous and the town of the same name probably has more 'Vente au détail/Dégustation' signs than any other in Provence. In the autumn there are traffic jams of flat-capped farmers hauling grapes by tractor to the presses, and the air itself is inebriating with a musty-sweet smell of freshly pressed grapes. The Mule-du-Pape restaurant stands on a corner overlooking this flow of grape traffic as it leaves the rows of vineyards on one side to pass the village fountain on the other. The restaurant started in the 1930s, first as a café and then as a country inn, serving meals cooked by the present owner's mother. At the same time other equally industrious members of the family were setting up a nougat firm in Montélimar and a wine firm in Châteauneuf.

· GIGOT d'AGNEAU et ses TARTELETTES d'AIL
leg of lamb with little garlic tarts (6)

1 LEG OF LAMB
2 GARLIC CLOVES, SLICED IN STRIPS
5 OR 6 ANCHOVIES, CUT IN PIECES
OLIVE OIL
SALT & FRESHLY GROUND BLACK PEPPER
10 GARLIC HEADS
3 TBSP/45 ML SINGLE/LIGHT CREAM
1 TBSP/15 ML TOMATO PURÉE
6 SMALL PRE-BAKED PASTRY SHELLS

A gigot of lamb at Easter in Provence has always been as common as Christmas turkey, and is often the Sunday roast served in Provençal restaurants. The anchovies and garlic used to stud the lamb in this recipe are as traditional as the whole branches of sage leaves that were once used as whisks, to dip in the pan juices and baste the lamb as it roasted.

At the Mule-du-Pape the cook anoints each slice of lamb with several creamy spoonfuls of puréed baked garlic. This heady infusion is also sometimes served in little pastry tart shells around the roast.

Preheat oven to 450°F/230°C/gas 8. Make small deep stabs with a pointed knife all over the lamb and press into them the slices of garlic and anchovies. Brush the lamb with olive oil and rub a very little salt and lots of ground pepper into the skin. Wrap the whole garlic heads in foil and place beside the roast. Place the roast on a rack over the vegetables (see next recipe), so the juices can drip through. Roast for the first 10 minutes in a very hot oven then turn the oven down to 375°F/190°C/gas 5 and continue roasting for 15–20 mins per lb/½ kg or until cooked to taste. Allow roast to rest in a warm place for 20 mins before carving. In the meantime make the sauce. Test garlic heads with the point of a knife. If not completely tender, place them in boiling water for 5–7 mins. When soft, cut the root ends of the whole garlic cloves and squeeze the paste into a bowl. Beat until creamy with 5–6 tbsp/75–90 ml pan juices from the tian, the thin cream and the tomato purée. (If you have had to boil the garlic some of its cooking liquid could be used to thin the sauce if necessary.) Add plenty of pepper (and salt, if needed). Spoon some of the sauce into the pre-baked pastry shells and serve them hot around the roast.

· TIAN de POMMES de TERRE ·
potato & tomato gratin (6)

This method of cooking crunchy and fragrant potatoes under a roast also works well with courgettes/zucchini instead. It owes its special taste to the fresh bay leaves tucked between the vegetables. If the roast is a small one the vegetables may have to be put in the oven before it.

6 MEDIUM POTATOES, PEELED
 AND SLICED IN THIN ROUNDS
6 MEDIUM TO LARGE TOMATOES,
 SLICED IN ROUNDS
4–6 FRESH BAY LEAVES CUT
 LENGTHWISE INTO STRIPS
FRESH THYME FINELY CHOPPED
SALT AND BLACK PEPPER
3–4 TBSP/45–60 ML COLD WATER
¼ PT/150 ML BOUILLON

Alternate potatoes with tomatoes in one layer in slightly over-lapping rounds in a shallow, well-oiled baking dish. Tuck strips of bay leaves between the vegetables and scatter thyme over the top. Season and sprinkle the cold water over the dish. Place directly beneath the roasting lamb. After 30 mins pour the bouillon over the vegetables and baste the lamb with the juices from time to time. Serve tian hot from its dish.

· CAILLETTES ·
spinach & pork terrine

A meal at the Mule-du-Pape begins with slices of spicy caillette, a cross between a sausage and a terrine famous in the Vaucluse region. The word comes from the Provençal 'gaio', meaning pork sweetbreads, but caillettes nowadays are usually made just with pork liver.

(Quantities for 12–18 small caillettes, to serve hot, or two large, to serve cold like a terrine.)

3 LB/1½ KG SPINACH, SWISS CHARD OR CURLY ENDIVE

1 LB/500 G PORK LIVER, COARSELY MINCED

1 LB/500 G BELLY PORK, COARSELY MINCED

1 LB/500 G LEAN SINEWLESS PORK, COARSELY MINCED

1 ONION, FINELY CHOPPED AND COOKED IN OLIVE OIL UNTIL SOFT

1 GOOD HANDFUL PARSLEY, FINELY CHOPPED

10 JUNIPER BERRIES, CRUSHED (OPTIONAL)

½ TSP/2.5 ML NUTMEG

SALT & PEPPER

1 SMALL WINEGLASS EAU-DE-VIE OR COGNAC

CAUL FAT (OR STRIPS OF UNSMOKED BACON IF NECESSARY)

½ PT/300 ML DRY WHITE WINE

12 SAGE LEAVES

Wash and then blanch the greens briefly in boiling water. Drain, rinse with cold water and squeeze out as much moisture as possible. Chop finely and mix well with all other ingredients except the caul, white wine and sage leaves. Form into 2 large or 12–18 small sausages and wrap each in a piece of caul (or bacon) previously softened for ½ hour in tepid water. Pour the wine into a shallow baking dish large enough to hold all the caillettes side by side. Lay the caillettes in the dish and into the top of each one press a sage leaf (or lay them side by side on the large caillettes). Bake for 45–60 mins, the first 20 mins at 450°F/230°C/gas 8, then at 400°F/200°C/gas 6. Baste often with the wine and if it dries up add a few tbsp warm water. Serve cold in slices with Mesclun or salade frisée à l'ail (page 130) or hot with a purée of chickpeas blended with the wine (reduced over high heat) from the caillettes.

Develop a close relationship with a good butcher – he is invaluable and will save you time and trouble in searching for specialist ingredients such as caul fat. This is a thin lacy membrane from the pig's intestines that adds richness to Provençal sausages and terrines without the extra fattiness of bacon.

Caul should always be soaked in tepid salty water first to soften it and then stretched as thinly as possible.

· VAISON-LA-ROMAINE ·

*V*aison-la-Romaine is really three towns: one not very ruined Roman, one medieval, climbing up a wooded hill to a 12th-century château, and one relatively modern – 18th and 19th-century. In Roman times, Vaison, one of the richest colonies in Provence, was filled with writers and merchants, the remains of whose houses, shops & gardens can still be seen. In the main square of the modern town there is the inevitable fountain where a man sits forever selling brochettes or crêpes or roast chestnuts, depending on the season, and a row of what in winter appears to be far too many outdoor cafés, even for Provence. In summer these are all full. And one at least attracts all the town's moped fans.

· FOUGASSE ·
sweet Provençal flat bread

In a corner of this square is an excellent boulangerie where they bake beautifully decorated breads & if requested will prepare plaited (braided) bread hearts, wrapped as 'paquets cadeaux'. Here as well there is 'fougasse', that curiously shaped bread found all over Provence, sometimes sweetened with orange-flower water (as it is in this recipe), but more often with pieces of bacon, onion or anchovy in the dough.

1 OZ/25 G FRESH YEAST
1 LB 2 OZ/500 G STRONG WHITE BREAD FLOUR, SIFTED
2 TBSP/30 ML ORANGE JUICE, TEPID
5 FL OZ/150 ML TEPID WATER
7 OZ/200 G CASTER SUGAR
4 TBSP/60 ML OLIVE OIL
2 EGGS, BEATEN

1 TBSP FENNEL SEEDS (OPTIONAL)

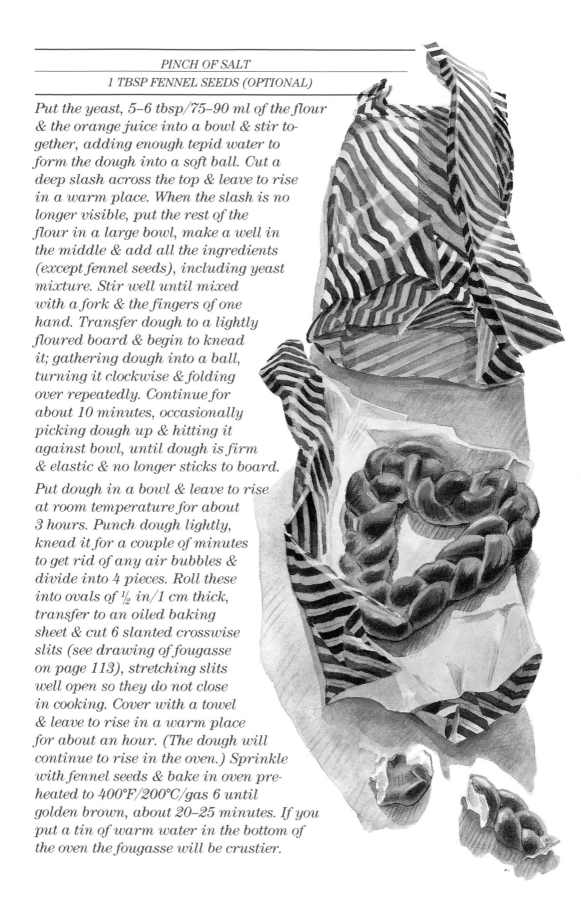

Put the yeast, 5–6 tbsp/75–90 ml of the flour & the orange juice into a bowl & stir together, adding enough tepid water to form the dough into a soft ball. Cut a deep slash across the top & leave to rise in a warm place. When the slash is no longer visible, put the rest of the flour in a large bowl, make a well in the middle & add all the ingredients (except fennel seeds), including yeast mixture. Stir well until mixed with a fork & the fingers of one hand. Transfer dough to a lightly floured board & begin to knead it; gathering dough into a ball, turning it clockwise & folding over repeatedly. Continue for about 10 minutes, occasionally picking dough up & hitting it against bowl, until dough is firm & elastic & no longer sticks to board.

Put dough in a bowl & leave to rise at room temperature for about 3 hours. Punch dough lightly, knead it for a couple of minutes to get rid of any air bubbles & divide into 4 pieces. Roll these into ovals of ½ in/1 cm thick, transfer to an oiled baking sheet & cut 6 slanted crosswise slits (see drawing of fougasse on page 113), stretching slits well open so they do not close in cooking. Cover with a towel & leave to rise in a warm place for about an hour. (The dough will continue to rise in the oven.) Sprinkle with fennel seeds & bake in oven preheated to 400°F/200°C/gas 6 until golden brown, about 20–25 minutes. If you put a tin of warm water in the bottom of the oven the fougasse will be crustier.

· VAISON MARKET ·

*O*n Tuesday mornings all of Vaison apart from the Roman ruins becomes a market. Stallholders who travel throughout the region come with their produce. Monsieur Gigodot from Nyons sells vegetable tarts that he makes in his farmhouse, and around the corner Spanish Carlos deep-fries sweet pastry churros to hand out in a twist of paper to a waiting line of children, just as he will at Nyons market on Thursday. Stalls are piled with cheeses from all over France, and although Provence is not a cheese-rich area (only ewe and goat cheeses are produced here) there are some local specialities – Banon from the mountain town of the same name, a chèvre/goat cheese that is wrapped in chestnut leaves and tied with raffia, and Picodon, a pungent chèvre from the nearby Drôme district.

· PICODONS À L'HUILE ·
goat cheeses in olive oil & herbs

It is the tiny bullet-hard Picodon that makes the best version of the Provençal speciality called 'chèvres à l'huile', in which goat cheeses are marinated for

up to a year in olive oil and herbs, a process that softens & enriches them.

1 CLOVE GARLIC

3 VERY SMALL SHALLOTS OR ONIONS

6–8 SMALL GOAT CHEESES (THE HARDEST AVAILABLE, PREFERABLY PICODON)

1 SPRIG EACH FRESH FENNEL, ROSEMARY, TARRAGON, THYME

1 TBSP/15 ML JUNIPER BERRIES

2 RED CHILI PEPPERS, CUT IN HALVES & DE-SEEDED

3–4 BAY LEAVES

1¼ PT/750 ML GOOD OLIVE OIL

Put the garlic & shallots at the bottom of a wide-necked glass preserving jar. Lay the goat cheeses on top with the sprigs of herbs interspersed between them. Push the berries, peppers & bay leaves down the sides in a decorative pattern, and cover completely with olive oil. Put the lid on and leave to marinate for at least one month in a cool place. Serve with crisp, bitter salads and crusty bread.

· *MAS DE BOUVEAU* ·

Between the Roman ruins of Vaison and the Roman ruins of Orange, the foothills of Mont Ventoux gradually disappear to become the Plain of Orange, flat as a copper crêpe pan. Mile after mile of vineyards stretch in all directions from the flat straight road, a road probably tramped by Hannibal and his elephants on the memorable invasion of Italy in 218 BC.

Smack in the middle of this plain is the pretty Mas de Bouveau, where the young chef transforms Picodons à l'huile (previous recipe) into Fromage de Chèvre Grillé sur Salade.

· FROMAGE de CHÈVRE · GRILLÉ sur SALADE
grilled goat cheeses on a bed of salad (6)

This dish is very good made with bitter leaves such as

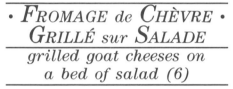

young dandelion leaves (called pissenlits, meaning piss-in-bed, because of their diuretic properties) or the mixture called Mesclun in Provence, available throughout the autumn & winter months in the markets & usually consisting of a quarter rocket/arugola leaves, a quarter red radicchio, a quarter young dandelion leaves and a quarter corn salad or lamb's lettuce/mâche.

1 HEAD CURLY ENDIVE,
   DANDELION LEAVES OR
   MESCLUN (AS ABOVE)

2 CLOVES GARLIC, PEELED &
   FINELY CHOPPED

3–4 FL OZ/75–100 ML
   OLIVE OIL

6 SMALL GOAT CHEESES
   IN OIL (AS ABOVE) OR SMALL
   FRESH GOAT CHEESES

6 PIECES LIGHTLY TOASTED
   FRENCH BREAD (SHOULD BE
   SLIGHTLY LARGER THAN
   CHEESE)

BLACK PEPPER

Wash & dry the salad and divide between 6 plates. Simmer garlic in oil until soft & golden. In the meantime put the cheeses on to the toasted French bread & place under a very hot grill for 5 mins. Transfer a grilled cheese to each plate & pour over a little of the hot garlic sauce. Season with black pepper & serve immediately.

· BROCHETTES de ROGNONS ·
d'AGNEAU
skewered lambs' kidneys (6)

Although rabbit is the Mas de Bouveau's speciality, grilled lambs' kidneys are also served, a recipe as old as wood fires in Provence. Years ago cooks either grilled the kidneys over vine wood or wrapped them in vine leaves before grilling.

12 LAMBS' KIDNEYS

1½ LB/700 G ROLLED SPARE RIB
   OR LOIN OF PORK, CUT IN ¾ IN/
   2 CM CUBES

2 RED PEPPERS

2 GREEN PEPPERS

6 SHALLOTS, PEELED & HALVED

1 LARGE GARLIC CLOVE, CRUSHED

SALT & PEPPER

4–5 TBSP/75 ML OLIVE OIL

ENOUGH VINE LEAVES TO WRAP
   EACH KIDNEY COMPLETELY

Remove transparent outer skin, then cut kidneys in ½ lengthwise & remove central core. Cut again, to quarter each kidney. De-seed peppers & cut them in 1 in/2.5 cm chunks. Mix together all ingredients except vine leaves, & marinate for several hours. Soak vine leaves in hot water 20 mins before grilling. Wrap kidneys securely in vine leaves. Assemble 6 skewers, alternating meat & vegetables. Grill for about 20 mins, turning skewers several times, brushing often with marinade.

· PETITS OISEAUX GRILLÉS ·
grilled small poultry
or game birds

The use of vine leaves is unusual in Provençal cookery.
This recipe comes from an old
Vaison cookery book, and
although originally meant for
very small grilled birds
(thrush, ortolan, etc), it is
very good for small poussins,
Rock Cornish hens, quail or
guinea fowl.

· FOR EACH BIRD ·
2 HEADS OF GARLIC

BRANCH OF FENNEL

HANDFUL BREADCRUMBS

1 TBSP/15 ML CRUSHED FENNEL
   SEEDS

SALT & PEPPER

OLIVE OIL

VINE LEAVES

2 RASHERS STREAKY BACON

HANDFUL GRAPES, SKINNED
   AND SEEDED

Assuming that the birds have
already been singed and
trimmed, wipe the insides
well with a damp cloth and
pat dry. Stuff with whole garlic (if used) and fennel leaves
and truss well. Mix breadcrumbs and fennel seeds
together and season with salt
and pepper. Brush each bird
with olive oil and then roll in
the crumb mixture. Cover
with vine leaves and bacon
and secure with thread or
string. Grill birds, brushing
them from time to time with
olive oil. Cook until juices
run clear when fattest part of
leg is pierced. Remove garlic
& leaves. Heat a little olive
oil, add grapes and stir for a
couple of minutes. Season
with salt and pepper and
serve separately with grilled
birds.

· FLAN de POMMES d'AMOUR ·
baked tomato custard (4)

This custard, with its pleasing
layers of green courgettes/zuc-
chini & red tomatoes, is very
good with roasts & poultry.

2 COURGETTES/ZUCCHINI, CUT IN
   ¼ IN/5 MM SLICES CROSSWISE

2 EGGS & 2 EGG YOLKS

1 TBSP/15 ML GOOD TOMATO COULIS

2 TBSP/30 ML CRÈME FRAÎCHE OR
   DOUBLE/HEAVY CREAM

2 TSP/10 ML FRESH TARRAGON,
   COARSELY CHOPPED

SALT & BLACK PEPPER

2 FIRM RIPE TOMATOES, CUT IN
¼ IN/5 MM SLICES.

Preheat oven to 350°F/180°C/
gas 4 & blanch courgettes.
Beat together eggs, tomato coulis, cream, tarragon, salt &
pepper. Grease 4 small metal
cocottes & into them layer
courgettes & tomatoes (alter-
nately). Divide the beaten egg
mixture between the four
dishes & place them in a bain-
marie or a shallow pan ½ full
of boiling water. Bake for
25–30 minutes or until set.
Turn out onto plates and serve
immediately.

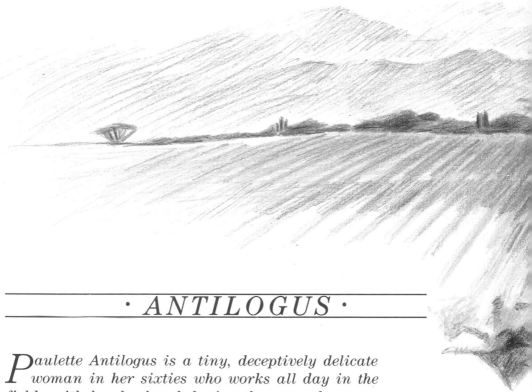

· ANTILOGUS ·

*P*aulette Antilogus is a tiny, deceptively delicate
woman in her sixties who works all day in the
fields with her husband during the grape harvest and then returns home to cook him a good
traditional meal. She and her family have always lived in the
big old farmhouse that looks down over vineyards to the
Roman town of Vaison, and beyond Vaison to the barren peak
of Mont Ventoux. On the next vineyard live her sister &
brother-in-law, the former as well-known a cook as Paulette,
the latter, with Paulette's husband, an inspired maker of the
local fortified wines – vin d'orange, vin de noix (made from
fresh green walnuts) and the almost lethal Farigoule, made
from wild thyme.

· VIN d'ORANGE ·
fortified orange wine

*Vin d'orange is served, as are
most sweet wines in Provence,
as an aperitif. It is also a
traditional Christmas and
New Year's treat.
(This recipe should make
approximately 4–5 bottles of
wine, depending on the juici-
ness of the oranges used. The
quantity can be halved,
although it is worthwhile
making enough to age.)*

*2¾ PT/1½ LITRES CÔTES DU RHÔNE
RED WINE (NO STRONGER THAN
11.5° OR 12° ALCOHOL)*

5 LARGE ORANGES, QUARTERED

*1 LEMON, CUT IN ½ IN/1 CM
SLICES*

1 VANILLA POD

½ TSP/2.5 ML GRATED NUTMEG

*10 OZ/280 G GRANULATED
SUGAR (APPROX)*

*½ PT/284 ML PURE FRUIT
ALCOHOL/EAU DE VIE (IF
AVAILABLE) OR POLISH PURE
SPIRITS (100°/120° PROOF) FROM
OFF-LICENCES/LIQUOR STORES*

Put lemon, oranges, nutmeg and vanilla pod into a large glass container with the red wine. Cork tightly and leave for 40 days. Filter through gauze or muslin and add 100 g sugar per 1¼ pt/ 1 litre of liquid. Let sugar dissolve and then add the pure fruit alcohol. Seal tightly again and leave for at least one month before drinking. This wine should be stored in a cool, dark place. It will continue to mature to a sherry-like consistency for about 3–4 years.

To make 'Liqueur de Farigoule' (farigoule is the Provençal word for thyme), fill a clean wine bottle ¾ full of fresh thyme. Cover with spirits (as used in previous recipe), cork tightly & leave for 2 months. Then boil 4 oz/100 g sugar with 8 fl oz/¼ litre water until syrupy. Sieve spirits & mix with syrup. Pour in litre bottle, cork, and drink after 2 mths.

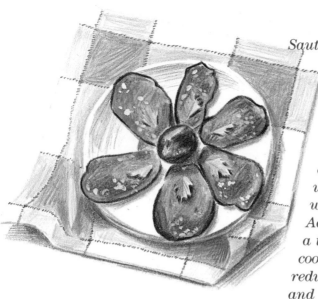

Sauté aubergine slices in hot oil until golden and tender on both sides. Drain well on paper towels. Add the garlic to the pan (with a little more oil if the aubergines have absorbed it all) and cook, until softened & golden, with some of the parsley. Add tomatoes and reduce to a thick purée. Stir in cheese, cook just until dissolved, then reduce heat & add cream, salt and pepper. Chill both tomato mixture & aubergines. Arrange aubergine slices in petal fashion on a large plate. Spoon some of the tomato mixture on to each slice & garnish with rest of parsley. Serve as a summer salad.

• AUBERGINES à la MARGUERITE •
aubergines/eggplant arranged like a daisy (4)

One of the delightful aspects of a Provençal meal, something noted by Elizabeth David in the fifties, is the series of small dishes that appears, each served as a separate course; like this one, in which Paulette's sister arranges slices of aubergine/eggplant to look like daisy petals.

2 LARGE EGG-SHAPED AUBERGINES/
  EGGPLANT, CUT LENGTHWISE
  INTO ½ IN/1.5 CM SLICES

OLIVE OIIL FOR FRYING

4 CLOVES GARLIC, PEELED AND
  FINELY CHOPPED

1 GOOD HANDFUL FRESH PARSLEY,
  FINELY CHOPPED

4–5 LARGE SWEET TOMATOES,
  PEELED, DE-SEEDED & CHOPPED

4 TBSP CREAM

6–8 TBSP/90–120 ML FRESHLY
  GRATED GRUYÈRE

SALT & PEPPER

• RÔTI de LAPIN avec •
ses PETITES SAUCISSES
rabbit roasted with its own little sausages (4)

So profusely does wild thyme grow in Provence that the poet Aubanel went into raptures on discovering Provençal shepherdesses whose feet were thyme-scented from walking barefoot through the fields. Of less poetic but more culinary interest: local rabbits, living on a regular diet of thymus vulgaris, need almost no extra seasoning. Paulette's recipe, however, will make even the blandest northern rabbit taste good.

1 4–5 LB/2–2.2 KG FRESH (NOT
    FROZEN) RABBIT, IF AVAILABLE,
    OR 2 2–2½ LB/1 KG RABBITS

• MARINADE •

½ PT/300 ML RED WINE

3 BAY LEAVES

2 TBSP/30 ML OLIVE OIL

3 CLOVES GARLIC, CRUSHED

1 MEDIUM ONION, FINELY
    CHOPPED

• STUFFING •

1 TBSP/15 ML COGNAC

1 HANDFUL BREADCRUMBS,
    SOAKED IN MILK & SQUEEZED OUT

1 CLOVE GARLIC, CRUSHED

2–3 OZ/75 G MUSHROOMS, FINELY
    CHOPPED

OIL FOR STUFFING

SMALL HANDFUL CHARD OR
    SPINACH, PARBOILED &
    FINELY CHOPPED

2 OZ/50 G BACON, MINCED

5 OZ/150 G SAUSAGEMEAT,
    MINCED

2 OZ/50 G VEAL OR LEAN BEEF,
    MINCED

LIVER & HEART OF RABBIT,
    FINELY CHOPPED (IF AVAILABLE)

1 EGG, BEATEN

SMALL HANDFUL THYME,
    FINELY CHOPPED

¼ TSP/1.25 ML NUTMEG

SALT & PEPPER

• FOR ROASTING •

1 TBSP/15 ML GRAIN MUSTARD

A FEW SPRIGS FRESH THYME

ENOUGH THIN RASHERS OF BACON
    TO COVER RABBIT

SALT & PEPPER

Marinate the rabbit for several hours, turning every hour. Preheat oven to 400°F/200°C/gas 6. Beat together the cognac, breadcrumbs and garlic & soften the mushrooms & onion in a little oil. Mix all the stuffing ingredients together very well. Remove rabbit from marinade (reserving marinade), pat dry and stuff lightly. (Don't pack stuffing in too tightly or it will not cook through.) Sew up the cavity & rub the skin with mustard. Lay the sprigs of thyme next to the skin, then wrap the rabbit in bacon rashers. Season in salt & pepper, then roast for about 1½ hours, or until juices from the densest part run clear. Baste every 20 minutes with juices from the pan, adding a little of the marinade if necessary.

When the rabbit is cooked, remove stuffing & leave until cool enough to handle, keeping rabbit warm meantime. Form stuffing into little sausages & place around roast. (If rabbit is to be served cold, place spoonfuls of stuffing on greaseproof paper, roll in a long cigar shape, chill, and slice when firm.) If serving rabbit hot, skim any excess fat from the pan, add strained marinade and reduce over a high heat to a syrupy consistency. Spoon over roast. Serve with a crisp, bitter salad of dandelion or endive.

· SÉGURET ·

*T*he Table du Comtat inn is built into the rock wall on a
narrow mountain road overlooking Séguret and the vineyards of the Plain of Orange. On Sundays and holidays it is
packed with local winegrowers and increasingly sophisticated
visitors. But however much the menu changes there is always
room on it for a few traditional Provençal dishes.

· PAPETON d'AUBERGINES ·
*Pope's aubergines/
eggplant (6)*

This is a melting aubergine
mousse that often appears in
Provençal homes, smacked
down on a bleached checked
tablecloth. The only garnish is
a dollop of rich tomato sauce
ladled over the top. At the
Table du Comtat restaurant
the Papeton is given a touch
of elegance the popes would
have approved of: individual
custards are served with a

delicious red pepper purée.
This recipe is a combination
of the rustic country recipe &
the Table du Comtat's more
elegant presentation.

2 LB/900 G AUBERGINES/EGGPLANT
SALT & PEPPER
3–4 TSP/50–60 ML OLIVE OIL
4 TBSP/60 ML GRATED GRUYÈRE
½ TSP/2.5 ML GRATED NUTMEG
2 TBSP/30 ML LEMON JUICE
4 IN/10 CM STRIP LEMON PEEL
¼ PT/150 ML MILK
2 EGGS & 2 EGG YOLKS
3 TBSP/45 ML DOUBLE/HEAVY CREAM
BUTTER

Preheat oven to 350°F/180°C/gas 4. Skin and slice the aubergines. Place in a colander, sprinkle lightly with salt and leave to stand for about an hour. Pat dry with paper towel, then cook the aubergines in olive oil in a non-stick pan until soft (about 25 mins). They will quickly absorb the oil, but it isn't necessary to add more. Cool, then push through a sieve or purée in an electric blender. Mix with the cheese, nutmeg and lemon juice. Heat the milk & lemon rind to just below boiling point & pour over the eggs, mixing well. Stir gently into the auber-gines, season, and spoon mixture into six individual greased ramekins. Dot with butter and bake in a bain-marie until set (about 25 mins). Turn out on to individual plates and serve lukewarm with a spoonful of red pepper purée.

* 1 November is 'La Toussaint', the first day of winter in Provence, the day that the year's new wines used to be decanted.

PURÉE de POIVRONS ROUGES
• red pepper purée •

½ MEDIUM ONION

1 CLOVE GARLIC

1–2 TBSP/20–30 ML OLIVE OIL

3 LARGE RED PEPPERS,
    DE-SEEDED & CHOPPED

2–3 SPRIGS FRESH THYME,
    FINELY CHOPPED

1½ PT/900 ML STOCK

SALT & PEPPER

Sauté the onion and garlic in oil until soft and golden. Simmer the peppers and thyme in stock until tender. Remove from stock, liquidize with onion and garlic and season to taste. If a more liquid sauce is preferred, add a little stock to dilute purée.

*F*ifteen kilometres north of Vaison-la-Romaine lies the town of Nyons, saved from the mistral's icier blasts by a protective circle of mountains. Its mild 'micro-climate' (as the locals proudly call it) is probably responsible for the excellence of Nyons olive oil, one of the best in the Midi. There are several olive oil mills in the town. One, the Huilerie du Pont Roman, stands next to a fifteenth-century humped-back stone bridge which curves gracefully over the River Eygues and from which the mill takes its name. Just down the road is La Scourtinerie, a beautiful 100-year-old factory in which Alain Fert sells local products and makes squashy pillow-shaped 'scourtins' – the hemp filters that have been used in oil, apple and honey presses since his grandfather invented the machinery to produce them in 1882.

*I*n 1956 a great frost destroyed almost all the olive trees in the country. As it takes five kilos of olives to make just one litre of pressed oil and ten years for an olive tree to become productive, 1956 could have been a disastrous year for the Fert family. Fortunately, Alain's grandfather remembered that old scourtins, too worn to filter oil, were often used as welcome mats; he began selling the new scourtins as rugs instead of oil filters. Now although Alain's scourtins still filter the olive oil in Provence's old fashioned mills, they also decorate floors all over France.

· ROUSTIDO dou MOULIN ·
oil mill grill

Up until the 1930s the oil millers used to offer their employees a casse-croûte of chunks of crusty bread that was moistened with olive oil and topped with garlic and crushed anchovies. When grilled golden over a fire this became Roustido dou moulin. Another practice was to chill olive oil until firm & spread it on bread, a practice that has continued unchanged since the '30s at the Restaurant Maurice Brun in Marseilles. Until the turn of this century, in fact, olive oil was always used raw, as a condiment rather than a cooking fat like butter.

· OLIVES MARINÉES ·
marinated olives

Alain Fert sells his own tiny, delicious Nyons olives, cured in a simple brine solution, the only treatment he considers necessary, or even acceptable, for high-quality olives. But not all olives are as perfect as those from Nyons: some can be improved by marinating. On one stall at the Nyons Thursday market there were 20 different varieties, some with bright yellow lemon halves or hot chili peppers; some mixed with brilliant wedges of sweet red, green and yellow peppers or feathery wild fennel; some 'olives aux herbes de Provence' cradled by great branches of fresh rosemary, thyme and savory.

1 LB/500 G BLACK OLIVES

1 PT/500 ML OLIVE OIL

1 SMALL ONION, CUT IN 8 PIECES LENGTHWISE

3–4 CLOVES GARLIC, CUT IN HALF

2–4 BAY LEAVES

1 BRANCH FENNEL

2 SPRIGS THYME

2 IN/5 CM STRIP ORANGE PEEL

10–12 CORIANDER SEEDS

Marinate all the ingredients together for at least 24 hours before serving. Serve in clear glass jars with the herbs pressed down the sides. If conserving for longer, store in covered crockery jars in a cool place.

· OLIVES CASSÉES ·
cracked olives

This method of preserving fresh green olives is excellent for people lucky enough to own a tree of even inferior olives. 'Casser' means 'to break or crack' and here refers to the blow the olives receive before treatment.

3 LB/1.5 KG FRESHLY PICKED GREEN OLIVES

5 PT/3 LITRES WATER (APPROX)

8 OZ/250 G SALT

1 BRANCH FENNEL

1 BRANCH BAY LEAVES

ZEST OF LARGE ORANGE

12 CORIANDER SEEDS

Crack but do not crush olives with a wooden mallet. Cover them with cold water in a glass jar and change the water every day for 9 days. Boil the last day's water with the other ingredients for 5 minutes. Let cool completly and pour over drained olives so they are all covered. (Add more water if necessary.) The olives are ready to eat after a week and will last a month or two if kept in a cool place.

· POUSSINS FARCIS ·
small chickens stuffed with olives (4)

Nyons olives are bluish-black, with large stones compared to the amount of flesh. Their taste is surpassed only by those from Beaumes-de-Venise, whose olive oil Alain Fert considers to be the best in Provence, not only because of the way it is made, but because the olives from that town are the best. Both are really too good for anything but eating straight out of the bowl. For the following recipe one Nyons olive vendor recommends using any ordinary meaty black olives, well drained and stoned/pitted. They make excellent stuffing for poultry.

2 SMALL CHICKENS OF 1½ LB/
750 G EACH OR 4 POUSSINS/
ROCK CORNISH GAME HENS OF
12–14 OZ/350–400 G

· STUFFING ·
THE CHOPPED GIBLETS (HEART,
GIZZARD, LIVER)
2 CLOVES GARLIC, FINELY
CHOPPED
2 SLICES BREAD, SOAKED IN
MILK & SQUEEZED OUT
6 OZ/150 G BLACK OLIVES,
STONED/PITTED & CRUSHED

· FOR COOKING ·
3 OZ/75 G UNSMOKED BACON,
FINELY CHOPPED
SALT & PEPPER
2 HEADS GARLIC, UNPEELED

Preheat the oven to 375°F/
190°C/gas 5. Mix all the
ingredients of the stuffing

thoroughly and stuff the birds. Sew up the cavities and truss well. Sauté the chopped bacon until the fat runs. Brush the birds with fat, season with salt and pepper and place in an oiled casserole (earthenware for preference) just big enough to hold both birds, breast side up. Push the garlic down between the birds and cook for about 30–40 minutes or until the juice from the thigh runs clear.

When the birds are cooked, either scoop out the stuffing and serve separately or cut the birds in half with poultry shears and leave the stuffing inside. Test the garlic heads with the point of a knife. If not completely tender, place in boiling water for 5–7 minutes. When soft, squeeze garlic into pan juices, stir well & spoon over the birds. Serve hot.

·FENOUIL à la TOMATE·
fennel baked with tomato

With these little stuffed chickens you might want to serve a simple dish of fennel baked with herbed tomatoes. Take one fennel bulb per person, quarter and core it; cook one finely chopped onion with some garlic, a handful of chopped fresh herbs and four plump, juicy tomatoes (or 1 large tin). When the tomatoes are reduced to a pulp, pour into an oiled ovenproof dish and arrange the fennel chunks in a circle on top. Seaon with salt and pepper, drizzle over a little olive oil and scatter with a few olives. Bake, covered, in a medium oven for 35–40 minutes. Serve hot or cold.

FRUITS OF THE GRAPE
NEAR AVIGNON

AT GIGONDAS: DOMAINE SAINT
  GAYAN (ROGER MEFFRE)
AT CHÂTEAUNEUF-DU-PAPE:
  DOMAINE DE MONTREDON &
  THE VIEUX MOULIN
AT VACQUÉRAS: LAMBERT FRÈRES
AT TAVEL: CHÂTEAU DE
  TRINQUEVEDEL (ROSÉ)
VINS DOUX NATURELS FROM
  BEAUMES-DE-VENISE AND
  RASTEAU

*I*n his *'Mémoires'* Frédéric Mistral described the Christmas Eves of his childhood in the sentimental nostalgic tones that only come with time and distance. First the perfect Yule log had to be found. And off in search of this *'bûche de Noël'* (which, to complicate matters, had to be made of fruitwood) trooped the whole family. Having found it, they carried it home and ceremoniously paraded around the kitchen three times in single file – Grandfather, Grandmother, Father, Mother, various and motley uncles, aunts and cousins, and little Frédéric bringing up the rear. Mistral's father then threw a glass of sweet, homemade *'vin cuit'* into the fire, followed by the Christmas log; with a cry of *'Bûche de Noël: mets le feu!'*, and the cheers of all the family, Christmas was welcomed to the house, and everyone sat down to eat.

*T*he Christmas Eve feast in Provence is not a Christmas-turkey-with-all-the-trimmings-but-one-day-early event. There is soup, there are all the little vegetable dishes that are so good in Provence, there is some fish, and then there is a grand collection (or not so grand, depending on the family) of 13 desserts to wind it all up before midnight mass. But no meat. The *'gros souper'* eaten on the 24th is, in short, more the trimmings without the beast. Most important in Mistral's day was *'le gros pain* calendal', the giant Christmas bread, a quarter of which was given to the first poor person who passed. And to each workman who came Mistral's mother gave a bottle of vin cuit and a napkin filled with bread, cheese, celery, sweet nougat and dried figs.

The Christmas celebrations have always begun on the 4th of December in traditional Provençal families; the day of Sainte-Barbe, when bowls of wheat and lentils are dampened, put near the warm chimney or stove, and left to sprout green shoots. These will form the grass in the Christmas crèche every day from the 24th to the 31st of December – except for the feasts on Christmas and Christmas Eve, when they rest on the table with the thirteen desserts. How well or badly these sprouts grow is said to indicate the future prosperity of the family. 'When the wheat grows well, all goes well.'

The crèche itself is an extraordinary sight, swarming with the little wood and clay figurines called 'santons', some beautifully carved, some painted by artists in a hurry so that their garishly-tinted eyes and mouths have slipped out of register under a too haphazard paint-brush. The traditional Nativity figures, often dressed in 19th-century Provençal costume, take their place beside more rustic French characters: gendarmes, Camarguais cowboys, drunkards, and olive-oil millers. Some of the larger crèches even have startling Hollywood lighting effects. At Séguret, near Vaison, there is a living crèche at the midnight mass, to which half of Provence seems determined to come, and recipes for all the traditional Christmas Eve dishes are chalked up on blackboards in the village.

·LE GROS SOUPER-ENTRÉES·

*O*n Christmas Eve the meal usually begins with a salad of celery or endive à l'anchoïade, or with escargots (and shiny new long nails to dig the reluctant ones out of their shells) and a bowl of aïoli. A soup may follow – Soupe de crouzets: little squares of pasta boiled in good bouillon and finished off under the grill with a liberal sprinkling of Gruyère and crushed walnuts – or aïgo boulido, which is no more than water perfumed with garlic and herbs. The Provençals say 'L'aïgo boulido sauvo la vido' ('l'aïgo boulido saves your life'). To this they add ironically 'Au bou d'un temps, tuio li gent' ('after a while it kills you'). It is after all, not a very substantial soup.

· L'AÏGO BOULIDO ·
garlic and herb soup (4)

There is an old recipe for Aïgo Boulido that says one should put some garlic and salt in a pot of water and let it boil the length of a couplet by the Provençal poet Saboly. This recipe is more exact, for those who haven't a handy copy of Saboly's poems in their kitchen.

6 CLOVES OF GARLIC,
   PEELED & CRUSHED
5 OR 6 SAGE LEAVES
1 BAY LEAF
1 TBSP/15 ML OLIVE OIL
1 EGG YOLK, BEATEN
SALT
FRESHLY GROUND BLACK PEPPER
4 PIECES OF TOAST
GRATED GRUYÈRE

Put the garlic and herbs in a saucepan with 2 pints/1 litre of water and the olive oil. Bring to the boil, simmer for 15 minutes and remove the herbs. Slowly pour the soup into the egg, beating vigorously. Season with salt and pepper, place the toast in 4 heated bowls and pour the soup over. Serve with grated cheese.

BOUILLABAISSE D'ÉPINARDS
spinach & egg soup (6)

The Provençals believe, and not without justification, that Provence is the only place fit for habitation. Given a sunny year, when the mistral has been notable by its absence, they are an unusually amiable people. But not when it comes to Bouillabaisse and what goes into a 'vrai Bouillabaisse', that famous Bouillabaisse that grandmère used to make. Tempers fray, voices rise, and the only fish that can be agreed on (of the 25 or so possibilities) is the strange spiny rockfish called rascasse. Then, of course, there must be onions and fennel and orange peel and saffron and ... Fortunately there is a bouillabaisse recipe which everyone agrees on – this spinach, potato and egg soup, which uses all the ingredients for the 'vrai Bouillabaisse'. Except for the fish – there are none. It comes from Marseilles and makes a good compromise between the soup and the vegetable dishes on Christmas Eve.

1 ONION, PEELED & DICED

3 CLOVES OF GARLIC, PEELED & CRUSHED

OLIVE OIL

2 LB/1 KG SPINACH, BLANCHED, SQUEEZED DRY & FINELY CHOPPED

6 SMALL POTATOES, PEELED & CUT IN ¼ IN/½ CM THICK ROUNDS

• BOUQUET GARNI •

BRANCH OF FENNEL

2 BAY LEAVES

GENEROUS SPRIG OF PARSLEY

PINCH OF SAFFRON

SALT & FRESHLY GROUND BLACK PEPPER

6 EGGS

6 PIECES OF TOAST

GRATED GRUYÈRE (OPTIONAL)

In a large saucepan cook the oinion and garlic in a little oil until softened. Add the spinach, toss well for 5 minutes and pile the potatoes, bouquet garni and saffron on top. Pour in 2 pints/1 litre of boiling water, season, cover and simmer over gentle heat. When the potatoes are tender, break the eggs, one by one into the soup and poach for 3 or 4 minutes. Ladle the broth over a piece of toast in each of 6 bowls, slip in a few slices of potato with an egg on top and serve with a big bowl of grated cheese.

· POISSONS ·

The fish on Christmas Eve may be mullet, tuna, bream or (most often) a dish of salt cod baked with spinach & garlic. In Arles they serve stuffed mussels with salty fougasse & bacon; at Maillane, Mistral's home near St Rémy, there is a dish of tiny squid called Tripes de mer – sea tripe

· MUGE aux OLIVES ·
grey mullet with olives (6)

This is a dish remembered by Mistral from childhood Christmas Eves in the 1830s. Although grey mullet is the fish used most often, the recipe works equally well with sea bass or red mullet.

1 GREY MULLET OF APPROX
   2½ LB/1 KG (OR 2 SMALLER
   FISH), CLEANED & SCALED

2 TBSP/30 ML FRESH FENNEL, DICED

½ LEMON, SLICED

2 BAY LEAVES

1 SMALL ONION, FINELY CHOPPED

2 CLOVES GARLIC, PEELED &
   SLIVERED LENGTHWISE

OLIVE OIL

1 TBSP/15 ML FLOUR, TOSSED WITH
2 TBSP/30 ML FINELY CHOPPED
   FRESH PARSLEY

HANDFUL OF SMALL BLACK
   OLIVES (STONED/PITTED
   IF YOU HAVE THE
   PATIENCE), NIÇOIS FOR
   PREFERENCE

3–4 TBSP/45–60 ML PASTIS OR
   WHITE WINE

SALT & PEPPER

Preheat the oven to 350°F/180°C/gas 4. Stuff the fish with

fennel, lemon and bay. In an oval flameproof dish (big enough to hold the fish) cook the onion and garlic in olive oil until tender. Roll the fish in flour and parsley and brown on each side in the pan. Add the olives, the wine or pastis and a sprinkling of salt and black pepper. Bubble for a few seconds, cover with a buttered sheet of greaseproof paper and bake for about 20 mins. Baste often during cooking and serve hot with lots of crusty bread.

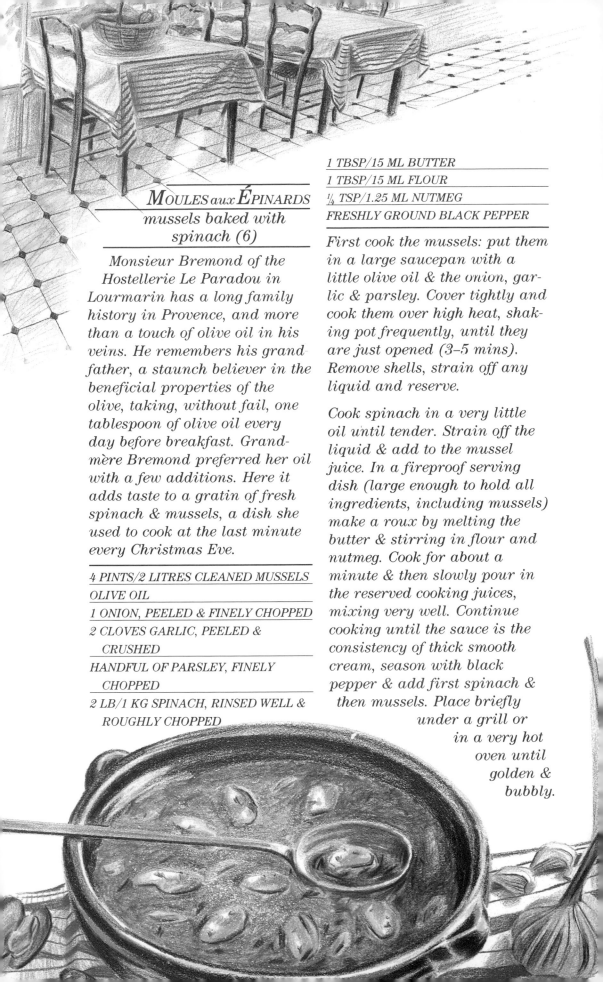

MOULES aux ÉPINARDS
mussels baked with spinach (6)

Monsieur Bremond of the Hostellerie Le Paradou in Lourmarin has a long family history in Provence, and more than a touch of olive oil in his veins. He remembers his grandfather, a staunch believer in the beneficial properties of the olive, taking, without fail, one tablespoon of olive oil every day before breakfast. Grandmère Bremond preferred her oil with a few additions. Here it adds taste to a gratin of fresh spinach & mussels, a dish she used to cook at the last minute every Christmas Eve.

4 PINTS/2 LITRES CLEANED MUSSELS
OLIVE OIL
1 ONION, PEELED & FINELY CHOPPED
2 CLOVES GARLIC, PEELED &
   CRUSHED
HANDFUL OF PARSLEY, FINELY
   CHOPPED
2 LB/1 KG SPINACH, RINSED WELL &
   ROUGHLY CHOPPED
1 TBSP/15 ML BUTTER
1 TBSP/15 ML FLOUR
¼ TSP/1.25 ML NUTMEG
FRESHLY GROUND BLACK PEPPER

First cook the mussels: put them in a large saucepan with a little olive oil & the onion, garlic & parsley. Cover tightly and cook them over high heat, shaking pot frequently, until they are just opened (3–5 mins). Remove shells, strain off any liquid and reserve.

Cook spinach in a very little oil until tender. Strain off the liquid & add to the mussel juice. In a fireproof serving dish (large enough to hold all ingredients, including mussels) make a roux by melting the butter & stirring in flour and nutmeg. Cook for about a minute & then slowly pour in the reserved cooking juices, mixing very well. Continue cooking until the sauce is the consistency of thick smooth cream, season with black pepper & add first spinach & then mussels. Place briefly under a grill or in a very hot oven until golden & bubbly.

·PETITS PLATS DE LÉGUMES·

*A*fter the fish appear all the little vegetable dishes – in Marseilles there is cauliflower salad and salsify in a gratin of cheese; near the Pont du Gard they serve a thick and creamy cabbage soup, and at Toulon an artichoke omelette. Two dishes are traditional all over Provence on Christmas Eve: Sauce d'épinards (a spinach gratin baked with hard-boiled eggs) and Sauce de cardes (swiss chard stalks baked with olives and anchovies), one of Paulette Antilogus' specialities.

· ENDIVES · au BEURRE d'ANCHOIS
chickory/Belgian endive with anchovy butter (6)

The anchovy butter in this recipe is a milder and creamier alternative to the stiff, and sometimes overwhelmingly fishy anchoïade sauce that is traditionally served with winter salads all over Provence. It contrasts well with the bitter crispness of the chicory.

5 ANCHOVIES (MORE IF YOU LIKE
   THEM A LOT)

4 TBSP/60 ML BUTTER PLUS
   ANOTHER 1 TSP/5 ML

1 TSP/5 ML FLOUR

1 TBSP/15 ML FRESH TARRAGON,
   FINELY CHOPPED (OR 1 TSP/
   5 ML DRIED)

JUICE OF ½ LEMON

BLACK PEPPER

6–8 HEADS CHICORY/BELGIAN
   ENDIVE, TRIMMED & HALVED

First pound the anchovies (washed in several changes of running water) with 4 tbsp/60 ml butter until smooth. Melt 1 tsp/5 ml butter in a frying pan over a low heat. When butter is golden (but definitely not brown) add the flour and tarragon and stir for a minute. Take the pan off the heat, mix in the lemon juice, pepper, and, little by little, the anchovy butter, stirring until smooth. Arrange the chicory on a dish and pour the sauce over them. Serve immediately.

· SAUCE de CARDES ·
gratin of swiss chard (6)

In the Lubéron and Vaucluse regions a 'sauce' is another name for a creamy vegetable stew enriched and bubbled brown in the oven. 'Cardes' are the stalks of mature swiss chard or 'blettes'.

Blettes 10

2 LB/1 KG SWISS
   CHARD STALKS,
   WASHED
   AND
   STRIPPED
   OF TOUGH
   STRINGS
   (OR CELERY, IF CHARD
   IS NOT AVAILABLE)

JUICE OF 1 LEMON

GLASS OF WHITE WINE

2 BAY LEAVES

SEVERAL SPRIGS OF
   THYME

1 ONION, FINELY
   SLICED

1 CLOVE OF GARLIC,
   PEELED AND
   CRUSHED

2 TBSP/30 ML OLIVE OIL

2 ANCHOVY FILLETS, CRUSHED

2 TBSP/30 ML FLOUR, SIFTED

3 TBSP/45 ML GRATED GRUYÈRE

¼ TSP/1.25 ML NUTMEG

SALT & PEPPER

HANDFUL OF SMALL BLACK OLIVES

Cut the chard into 1 in/2.5 cm pieces and boil for 20 minutes with lemon juice, wine, bay leaves, thyme & enough water to just cover. In a flameproof dish (big enough to hold all the ingredients) soften the onion and garlic in the olive oil, stir in the anchovies, and sprinkle the flour over. Stir for a minute or two and then begin to add the strained, still-warm liquid from the chard little by little, mixing well until it is the consistency of thickish cream. Let simmer for 10 mins and add the cheese, nutmeg, salt (if necessary), pepper and chards. Scatter with olives and place in a hot oven until pale golden and bubbling.

* To use this recipe for a dish of spinach or swiss chard tops, cook 2 lb/1 kg of the washed vegetable in 8 fl oz/225 ml water until tender. Drain & chop it & continue as above.

· LES TREIZE DESSERTS ·

*T*he Christmas Eve feast, having begun simply, always ends with the extravagant-sounding Thirteen Desserts – which may in fact be quite modest offerings. Amongst the poor families of Provence these desserts were once just dried fruits and nuts common to the countryside, a tradition that lingers on in what are now called the 'four beggars' – dried figs, raisins, almonds and walnuts. There are usually dates and 'pompe à l'huile' – Provençal brioche made with olive oil dough, traditionally served at Christmas – as well, trays of nougat noir and beautifully shaped pâte de coings, a dense, sweetened paste of baked quinces. Then in each town there are specialities: in Aix, the almond paste sweets called 'calissons'; in Nice, a sugared pie of swiss chard and pine nuts; in Vaison and the Drôme, fruit tarts such as the apple Panade cooked by Paulette Antilogus; in Haute Provence, cakes of chestnuts and dried fruits; and in Séguret, the delicious cornmeal cake called 'Lou Mias'.

· LOU MIAS ·
cornmeal Christmas cake

This moist cornmeal cake would once have been made with goats' milk and baked on a hot griddle in the fireplace. A modern oven gives more reliable results.

8 FL OZ/225 ML MILK
7 OZ/200 G SUGAR
JUICE AND GRATED ZEST OF 1 ORANGE
9 OZ/250 G FINE-GRAINED YELLOW CORNMEAL
PINCH OF SALT
4 EGGS
3 TBSP/45 ML OLIVE OIL
ICING SUGAR

Heat the milk to boiling, lower the heat and mix in sugar and peel, stirring until the sugar dissolves. Remove from heat and stir, little by little, into the cornmeal with a fork. Add salt and stir in orange juice. Leave in a warm place for ½ an hour. Beat in eggs one by one and add oil. Heat oven to 400°F/200°C/gas 6. Pour mixture into a well-buttered, lined round cake tin and bake for about 35–40 minutes or until a knife inserted into the cake's centre comes out clean. Let cool for 10 minutes and turn out on to a rack. Dust lightly with icing sugar and serve with home-made orange wine (page 134).

Apt's famous glacé fruit is sold in special mixes – intended to be soaked for several months in eau-de-vie & brought to the Christmas table, plump & tipsy with good spirits.

·Panade/Tarte de Noël·
grated apple & orange Christmas tart

In Séguret the older cooks make this pie as they always have done: with the orange-scented Fougasse dough on page 126 sprinkled with extra orange flower water after cooking. Paulette Antilogus, further north in Vaison la Romaine, prefers the crunchier texture of shortcrust pastry. Both are good.

SHORTCRUST PASTRY
8 OZ/250 G PLAIN WHITE FLOUR
PINCH OF CINNAMON
4 OZ/125 G BUTTER, TAKEN FROM THE FRIDGE AN HOUR BEFORE USE

• FILLING •

3 OZ/80 G (APPROX) BUTTER

3 LB/1.4 KG GOLDEN DELICIOUS
   APPLES*, PEELED, CORED
   AND GRATED

JUICE & GRATED ZEST OF
   1 ORANGE

2 TBSP/30 ML HONEY

A LITTLE SUGAR TO FINISH

* IF YOU USE BRAMLEYS OR OTHER
TART GREEN APPLES, ADD 4 OZ/
100 G SUGAR.

If not using fougasse, make shortcrust pastry. Sift flour and cinnamon together in a bowl. Cut the butter into hazelnut-sized lumps and rub into the flour with fingertips until mixture resembles fine breadcrumbs. Sprinkle a little cold water over the surface and mix with a knife until dough leaves sides of bowl clean. Roll dough into a ball free from cracks. Chill for at least 1 hour. Meanwhile melt remaining butter in a heavy frying pan, add apples, orange zest, juice & sugar and cook until softened, stirring constantly. When most of the juice given off by the apples has evaporated, stir in the honey, remove from heat & chill. Roll out pastry to about ¼ in/4 mm thick, saving about a third to make a lattice top. Line an 8–9 in/20–22.5 cm buttered pie dish with the pastry, prick the base with a fork and chill again, together with pastry for lattice, for 30 minutes. Preheat oven to 400°F/200°C/gas 6. Fill the pastry with apple mixture, make a lattice top and bake on a hot baking sheet for 20–25 minutes until golden and crisp. While still warm sprinkle with sugar.

ADDITIONS:

In the Drôme district north of Séguret 'panades' are made at Christmas with a variety of fillings, replacing the pompe à l'huile common to Marseilles. The following ingredients may be substituted for the grated apples in the above recipe (but traditional panade should always have a lattice top):

EQUAL PARTS GRATED APPLES
   AND PEARS

THINLY SLICED APPLES WITH
   3–4 SPOONFULS OF MELTED
   LAVENDER HONEY & A
   HANDFUL OF TOASTED,
   CHOPPED WALNUTS

1¼ LB/500 G PUMPKIN OR
   MARROW/GIANT ZUCCHINI,
   BLANCHED & SHREDDED,
   MIXED WITH 6 OZ/150 G SUGAR,
   A TSP OF VANILLA ESSENCE
   AND A HANDFUL OF
   TOASTED ALMONDS, FINELY
   CHOPPED

THE SAME QUANTITY OF
   APPLES, GRATED RAW ON
   TO THE PASTRY, SPRINKLED
   WITH SUGAR AND A FEW
   SPRINKLES OF ORANGE
   FLOWER WATER

| 8 OZ/250 G SUGAR |
| 1 SMALL GLASS COLD WATER |
| 1 TBSP/15 ML ORANGE FLOWER WATER |
| 8 OZ/250 G HONEY (LAVENDER IF POSSIBLE) |
| 3 EGG WHITES, BEATEN STIFF |
| 7 OZ/200 G ALMONDS, PEELED, HALVED & TOASTED |
| 4 OZ/100 G PISTACHIOS, PEELED AND TOASTED |
| 4 OZ/100 G MIXED CANDIED PEEL |

· NOUGAT BLANC ·
mixed fruit and nut nougat with egg whites

The most famous nougat in the world comes from Montélimar, just north of Provence. But the most interesting place to buy real Provençal nougat is the lovely windy village of Sault in the wild hills east of Mont Ventoux. Every window in every shop seems to be selling nougat – or the honey and lavender from which it is made. Even the local hatshop displays its wares on stands of honeypots!

Over a gentle heat melt the sugar with the water and orange flower water in a heavy-based pan. Melt the honey in another, stirring it constantly with a wooden spoon. When a drop of honey in cold water can be formed into a soft ball and a drop of sugar syrup into a hard ball, remove from heat and mix the sugar syrup into the honey. Immediately fold in the egg whites until well blended. Return this to the heat and continue cooking and stirring over low heat. When the nougat is very thick and matt white – this may take about 45 minutes! – stir in the nuts and fruit little by little, having first warmed them in the oven for about 10 minutes. Pour the nougat into a well-oiled pan, about ¾ size but same depth as for nougat noir (see following recipe), lined with rice paper. Slice into squares and serve lukewarm.

· NOUGAT NOIR ·
honey & almond nougat

Although the famous Montélimar white nougat is likely to come from a commercial factory, this black 'nougat noir' is a common Christmas Eve treat, handmade in most Provençal homes.

| 1 LB/500 G WHOLE ALMONDS, PEELED |
| 1 LB/500 G HONEY |
| GRATED ZEST OF ½ ORANGE |

Pour the honey into a heavy-based saucepan over a very gentle heat and stir steadily with a wooden spoon. When the honey begins to bubble throw in the almonds and orange zest. Continue stirring until the almonds start to crack and turn golden in the middle and the honey is dark brownish-black. Remove from heat, continue to stir until tepid and pour into a well-oiled pan (about 9 × 6 × 1½ in/24 × 15 × 3.5 cm) lined with rice paper. Cover with more rice paper and a weighted board of the same size as the inside of the pan. Refrigerate and slice into small squares when completely cool.

Occasionally it is possible to find old-fashioned nougat pans with spring-release sides and bases. This makes it considerably easier to remove the nougat from its pan for slicing.

Even devotees of sugared quince paste 'pâte de coing', another Provençal Christmas speciality, may find it laborious to make. St Rémy produces an excellent plain commercial version and for more opulent jellies (see illustration page 154) Avignon's confiseries are the best in the country.

· INDEX ·

Recipes are indexed according to their English names

MONTÉLIMAR

D   A   U   P   H

Nyons

Vaison·la·Romaine

Séguret
Gigondas

ORANGE

Châteauneuf
·du·Pape

Cabrières
d'Avignon

Gordes

Viens

Ch
Ar

AVIGNON

Oppède

Ménerbes

Apt

L U B É R O N

D

RHÔNE

St. Rémy·
·de·Provence

Lourmarin

Les
Baux

Maussane

Eygalières

Méjanes

ARLES

P

Puyfond

Aigues
Mortes

R

AIX·EN·PRO

O   V

Les
Stes. Maries
de la Mer

MARSEILL

Cassis

M

É

D   I   T